# THE
# CURRY
## COOKBOOK

# THE CURRY COOKBOOK

## Charmaine & Reuben Solomon

RAINCOAST BOOKS

*Vancouver*

First published in Canada in 1995 by
Raincoast Book Distribution Ltd.
8680 Cambie Street
Vancouver, B.C. V6P 6M9
(604) 323-7100

Produced by Lansdowne Publishing Pty Ltd
Level 5, 70 George Street, Sydney 2000, Australia

First published by Lansdowne Press 1980
Published in Windward edition for W.H. Smith & Son Limited 1982
This edition first published 1995

**Canadian Cataloguing in Publication Data**

Solomon, Charmaine.
The curry cookbook

Includes index.
ISBN 1-895714-99-0.

1. Cookery (Curry)  I. Solomon, Reuben.  II. Title.
TX819.C9S64 1995     641.6'384     C95-910696-0

Original photographers: Ray Joyce, Reg Morrison
Additional photography for this edition: Geoff Lung
Cover photograph by Geoff Lung
Designed by Kathie Baxter Smith

Printed in Hong Kong by South China Printing Co.

PHOTOGRAPHS:
*Front of jacket and half-title page: Green Curry of Fish, recipe page 48.*
*Opposite title page: Red Curry of Beef, recipe page 30.*

# CONTENTS

~

# ACKNOWLEDGEMENTS

I WOULD LIKE to thank the following for their part in providing artefacts, utensils, and ingredients used in photography: The Tourist Organisation of Thailand, The Thai Trade Centre, The Indian Tourist Office, Mrs Ida Htoon Phay, The NSW Fish Marketing Authority.

But most of all I want to thank my husband, Reuben, whose help I enlisted in the preparation of this book and who has worked very hard to make it good. He really is the greatest curry enthusiast I know and has a flair for creating dishes with a clever use of spices. Why waste such talent? He has learned to walk a fine line between his carefree improvisations as a cook and the careful measuring and committing to paper, to which every cookery writer must submit. And so, when you enjoy the results of your cooking from these recipes, I cannot take all the credit – Reuben take a bow!

# BASICS OF CURRY COOKING

*In most curries, besides spices, there are ingredients you will be
using repeatedly so let's become familiar with them.*

**Onions:** Almost every curry includes onions. In Asia, the onions are mainly purplish red, rather like the true shallot, the small bulb that grows in clusters like garlic. Since these are not always available we have used brown or white onions. These vary so much in size that for guidance in helping you decide what we mean by a large or medium onion, a large onion is 8 oz (250 g) or more; a medium onion is about 4 oz (125 g) and a small onion is around 60 g (2 oz). The next time you buy onions, weigh some of different sizes to obtain an idea of the variation. But don't bother to weigh your onions each time you cook a curry. It's not all that crucial.

**Garlic:** Garlic cloves can vary from tiny ones the size of a pistachio nut to big ones about the size of a walnut! To introduce uniformity we adopted the method of chopping garlic and measuring it in spoonfuls. Since the garlic is usually chopped anyway before cooking, this does not entail extra work.

**Ginger:** The Asian way of calling for a slice or two of ginger, or a "thumb-sized" piece of ginger gives too much leeway so again we have called for chopped or grated ginger root, measured in standard spoons.

**Chilies, Fresh:** Fresh chilies are used in most Asian food. For mild curries, the whole chili is added while simmering, then lifted out and discarded. But for an authentic fiery quality the chilies should be chopped or perhaps ground in the electric blender. If you leave the seeds in the flavor will be hotter than if you remove the seeds. Either way, equip yourself with disposable plastic gloves or well-fitting rubber gloves because chilies can be so hot that even repeated washings will not stop the tingling sensation that will result if your skin comes into contact with the juices.

Having protected your hands, remove stalk of chili and make a slit to remove the seeds, scraping them out with the tip of a knife. Or cut the chili in two lengthways and remove the central membrane together with the seeds. Remember, do not touch your face, your eyes or young children after handling chilies – it is an experience you won't forget!

**Chilies, Dried:** There are large and small dried chilies. The smaller they are, the hotter they are. Those called for in these recipes are the large variety, and they still have plenty of heat and flavor.

Break off the stem and if you don't want too much heat, shake so the seeds fall out. Soak for 10 minutes in hot water before grinding. Dried chilies, though they give plenty of oomph, do not have as much effect on the skin as fresh chilies with their volatile oils.

Until they have been soaked and ground they are safe enough to handle. But following this process, remember to wash your hands at once with soap and water.

*Coconut Cream:* There are so many ways to get coconut cream other than from a fresh coconut... canned, concentrated or "creamed" coconut, frozen and so on.

For convenience you may use canned coconut cream for the recipes in this book. Make sure, however, that it is unsweetened and that you purchase a good brand. It should be white in color, not grey. And the smell should be fresh and sweet. Not all canned coconut creams are created equal. Be choosey. The concentrated creamed coconut is also convenient and should be dissolved in water: about 2 oz (60 g) creamed coconut and enough water to make up 1 cup (8 fl oz, 250 ml) makes a medium strength coconut cream. Use more for "thick" cream and less for "thin" cream.

One of the best and most reliable methods is extracting coconut cream from unsweetened desiccated coconut (dried, shredded coconut).

Coconut cream is extracted in two stages. The first yield being the "thick" cream, the second "thin" cream. Use a mixture of first and second extracts when a recipe calls for coconut cream, unless thick cream or thin cream is specified. Sometimes they are added at different stages of the recipe. In some recipes you use "thick coconut cream". This is the rich layer that rises to the top of the thick cream (or first extract) after it has been left to stand for a while. If the coconut cream is to be cooked down to make an oily substance, as for instance in the Thai curry pastes, read the label on the canned coconut cream, as it may contain a stabilizer and instead of turning to oil you end up with crunchy brown bits of dried coconut cream which are very nice to nibble, but totally unsuitable for the purpose of the recipe.

*Using desiccated coconut:* Put 2 cups (16 oz, 500 ml) desiccated coconut in a large bowl and pour $2^1/2$ cups (20 fl oz, 600 ml) hot water over. Allow to cool to lukewarm, then knead firmly with your hand for a few minutes and strain through a fine strainer or a piece of muslin, squeezing out as much liquid as possible. This should yield about $1^1/2$ cups (12 fl oz, 375 ml) thick coconut cream.

Using the same coconut and $2^1/2$ cups (20 fl oz, 600 ml) more hot water, repeat the process. Knead well and squeeze really hard to get all the moisture and flavor from the coconut. This will yield approximately 2 cups (16 fl oz, 500 ml) thin coconut cream. (Because of the moisture retained in the coconut after the first extract, the second extract usually yields more cream.)

*Using a blender:* With an electric blender you save time and a lot of hard kneading and squeezing. Put 2 cups (16 fl oz, 500 ml) desiccated coconut and $2^1/2$ cups (20 fl oz, 600 ml) hot water in blender container, cover and blend for 30 seconds on high speed. Strain through a fine sieve or piece of cheese cloth (muslin), squeezing out all the moisture. Repeat process, using the same coconut and $2^1/2$ cups (20 fl oz, 600 ml) more hot water.

*Using fresh coconut:* In Asian countries, fresh coconut is used. It may be bought ready grated from the markets, but a coconut grater is standard equipment in every household. If you can buy a coconut grater at one of the Asian stores, well and good. If you can't, the blender comes to the rescue again.

Let's start with the coconut. First crack in two by hitting it with the back of a heavy kitchen chopper on the middle of the nut. Tap hard several times, going round the "equator" of the coconut. Once a crack has appeared, insert the thin edge of a blade and prise it open. Save the sweet liquid for drinking. (This is not coconut milk, though it is commonly referred to as such in western books.) Put the two halves of the nut into a low oven and in 15 or 20 minutes the flesh will start to come away from the shell. Lift out with the point of a knife, peel away the thin dark brown skin that clings to the white meat. Cut into chunks, put into an electric blender with 2 cups (16 fl oz) water and blend at a high speed until coconut is pulverized. Strain out liquid, repeat using more water and same coconut.

To extract fresh coconut cream by hand, grate the pieces of white meat finely and to each cup of grated coconut add 1 cup (8 fl oz, 250 ml) of hot water, knead thoroughly and strain out the liquid. Repeat process a second and even a third time, adding hot water.

# PRESENTATION
# OF CURRY

JUST AS FAR EASTERN food tastes better when eaten with chopsticks, so the food of India and South East Asia tastes better eaten with the fingers. Rice or unleavened bread is most often served with spicy curries and other accompaniments. And the only way to manage the flat breads is by tearing off pieces and using them to scoop up the curries. Rice is usually served with spoon and fork, though the purists prefer to use the fingers of the right hand. There is a knack to it which may need a little practice for the novice.

More important than "how to" is "how much". In other words, a good meal is mainly a matter of proportions, and this is where the inexperienced Westerner comes undone. In western meals it is the meat, fish, or poultry which is the main item. In Asian meals, rice or bread such as chapatis or rotis form the main part of the meal, while the spicy curries and accompaniments are meant to be eaten in smaller quantities. Certainly there should be three or four times as much rice as curry for the spiciness of curry is cushioned by the neutral rice and no discomfort is felt afterwards. If rice is relegated to a minor role the richness of the curries may prove too much for the average digestion.

All the food is brought to the table at once. Rice should be served with a meat or poultry curry, with a fish or other seafood curry and with two or more vegetable curries. On festive occasions beef, pork, chicken, prawns are served at the same meal, each one prepared in a different style. Accompaniments are served in smaller quantities, and indeed, the more pungent and strongly flavored they are, the smaller the amount that should be placed on the table and the smaller the spoon should be to serve them. Some very hot sambals we serve with a coffee spoon as an indication these are only the accents to the meal and should be approached with caution. But if your guests are not accustomed to Asian food, don't rely on the subtle hint of small portions and spoons; come right out and warn them that such and such a dish is hot with chilies or they may find themselves in much discomfort.

Pappadams, the popular lentil wafers which are served with Indian or Sri Lankan meals, should always be placed on a separate small plate like a bread and butter plate. Otherwise the steam from the hot food will cause their delightful crispness to diminish.

Etiquette (and commonsense) decree that rice is served first in the middle of the plate. Curries and accompaniments are placed around it in much smaller quantities. The impression that rice and all the curries should be mixed together is quite wrong. Each different accompaniment or curry should be tasted separately, with a mouthful of rice or piece of chapati.

What to drink with a curry meal? Cool water is ideal. If you prefer an alcoholic beverage, please consider ice-cold beer or other light ale. A beer shandy is particularly nice.

For wine drinkers, a light wine punch such as sangria is delicious or a very fruity white wine. Avoid dry wines, particularly red wines. Fine wines are lost when served with highly spiced food and a dry wine does nothing to complement a good curry.

Or serve mango juice or rose-flavored syrup poured over crushed ice. It is ideal for sipping with a curry meal.

# Curry Pastes & Spice Combinations

WE DO NOT recommend using a standard curry powder because it will produce a sameness in all your curries. But certain combinations of fragrant spices, herbs, and whole, unground seeds add such a marvellous aromatic accent, they are very useful to have on hand.

For instance, the combination of five seeds (panch phora) used in Indian cooking is all that is necessary to transport a vegetable from blandness to sheer delight. The seeds, combined in certain proportions and used whole, not ground, are tossed in a small quantity of hot oil or ghee to release the flavors which then permeate the vegetable during cooking.

Then there are the ground spice mixes (garam masalas) which emphasize and enhance the flavors. They are impractical to make in the very small amounts called for in each recipe, so I advise grinding a quantity and storing it airtight and away from heat and light. It will retain its flavor and fragrance for months if stored in the freezer.

The fresh herbs used in green masala paste are not always in season, and one should therefore prepare a few bottles when they are available. This preserves them in oil for use later on. Green masala paste may be used to add a flavor change to basic Indian curries, or it may be used on its own.

As you use this book you'll find that while some of the spices are common to the cooking of most Asian countries, there are others that are very definitely confined to one area. This applies particularly to fresh herbs such as fenugreek (popular in India but not in South East Asia). On the other hand, lemon grass (serai) and pandan (rampé) which are almost universally used in South East Asian cuisine and even in Sri Lanka which is so close, geographically, to India, are never used in Indian food.

Even different parts of the same plant are favoured according to the country we visit. The fresh green leaves of coriander herb are found in the cooking of India, and all the way east to China, except in Sri Lanka where it is looked upon with disfavor because of its pungent smell. But in Thailand, where the root of the plant is used in combination with garlic and black pepper, this is considered of greater importance than the leaves.

Although we would never advocate using the same spice mixture for any and every curry, for convenience a small amount of a good curry powder does come in handy. You can, of course, buy one. Many good mixtures are sold commercially, but there are also many that lack flavor because of a skimping on the more expensive spices and a reliance on "fillers" such as rice flour, to make up the bulk. "Curry powder" is scorned in Asian countries, housewives and cooks preferring to make their own combinations.

When buying a commercial curry powder, check that it comes in tins or bottles and is not packed in cardboard or plastic. Much of the flavor and aromatic oils are quickly dissipated when packed in those materials.

If you are pressed for time and wish to have a curry meal, use a good curry paste or a commercial curry powder, but do not stop at that.

By adding small quantities of your favorite spices you will enhance and vary the flavor of that particular curry powder.

Making your own curry powder is vastly more satisfying if you are a true curry enthusiast – and you must be, or you would not be reading this. We are including recipes for some curry blends, but even if you like them very much do remember these are not to be relied on every time you cook a curry.

Curries and other spiced dishes must have distinctive character. This is the reason why we have mostly used individual spices in the recipes that follow. When cooking a curry, the cook with his or her spices is like an artist with a palette full of colors, mixed together to create a masterpiece.

In this book we have given you our own special recipes for the curries. Use them as a starting point, because we've tested them and found that's how we like them. But by all means feel free to be the artist the second time around, and improvize. We wish you happy cooking and good eating.

*INDIA*

# PANCH PHORA

∞

*"PANCH" MEANS FIVE IN HINDI, AND PANCH PHORA IS A COMBINATION OF FIVE DIFFERENT AROMATIC SEEDS. THESE ARE USED WHOLE AND, WHEN ADDED TO THE COOKING OIL IMPART A FLAVOR TYPICAL OF CERTAIN INDIAN DISHES.*

2 tablespoons black mustard seed
2 tablespoons cumin seed
2 tablespoons black cumin seed
1 tablespoon fenugreek seed
1 tablespoon fennel seed

Put all ingredients into a glass jar with a tight-fitting lid. Shake before using to ensure an even distribution.

*SRI LANKA*

# CEYLON CURRY POWDER

∞

1 cup (3 oz, 90g) coriander seeds
$1/2$ cup ($1^1/2$ oz, 45g) cumin seeds
1 tablespoon fennel seeds
1 teaspoon fenugreek seeds
1 cinnamon stick, about 2 in (5 cm)
1 teaspoon whole cloves
1 teaspoon cardamom seeds
2 tablespoons dried curry leaves
2 teaspoons chili powder, optional
2 tablespoons ground rice, optional

In a dry pan over low heat roast separately the coriander, cumin, fennel and fenugreek, stirring constantly until each one becomes a fairly dark brown. Do not let them burn.

Put mixture into blender container together with cinnamon stick broken in pieces, the cloves, cardamom, and curry leaves. Blend on high speed until finely powdered. Combine with chili powder and ground rice if used. Store in an airtight jar.

*INDIA*

# GARAM MASALA

∞

*SPRINKLE A TEASPOON OF THIS OVER A CURRY BEFORE SERVING — THE RESULT IS BREATHTAKING. REUBEN.*

4 tablespoons coriander seeds
2 tablespoons cumin seeds
1 tablespoon whole black peppercorns
2 teaspoons cardamom seeds (measure after removing pods)
4 x 3 in (7.5 cm) cinnamon sticks
1 teaspoon whole cloves
1 whole nutmeg

In a small pan roast separately the coriander, cumin, peppercorns, cardamom, cinnamon, and cloves. As each one starts to smell fragrant turn on to a plate to cool. Put all ingredients into electric blender and blend to a fine powder. Finely grate nutmeg and mix in. Store in a glass jar with an airtight lid.

*INDIA*

# MADRAS CURRY PASTE

∞

1 cup ($2^2/3$ oz, 80g) ground coriander
$1/2$ cup ($1^1/3$ oz) ground cumin
1 tablespoon each ground black pepper, turmeric, black mustard, chili powder, and salt
2 tablespoons each crushed garlic and finely grated fresh ginger
vinegar for mixing
$3/4$ cup (6 fl oz, 180ml) oil

Combine ground spices and salt in a bowl. Add garlic and ginger and sufficient vinegar to mix to a smooth, thick purée. Heat oil in saucepan and when very hot turn in the spice mixture and reduce heat. Stir constantly until spices are cooked and oil separates from spices. Cool and bottle.

Use about a tablespoon of this paste for each 1 lb (500 g) of meat, fish or poultry, substituting it for the garlic, ginger and spices in a recipe.

*THAILAND*

# GREEN CURRY PASTE

∾

4 large fresh green chilies

1 teaspoon black peppercorns

1 small brown onion, chopped

1 tablespoon chopped garlic

2 tablespoons chopped fresh coriander plant,
root and leaves

1 stem fresh lemon grass, sliced or
2 teaspoons chopped lemon rind

1 teaspoon salt

2 teaspoons ground coriander

1 teaspoon ground cumin

1 teaspoon serai powder

1 teaspoon laos powder

2 teaspoons dried shrimp paste

1 teaspoon ground turmeric

1 tablespoon oil

Remove stems of chilies, leaving in the seeds if you want the curry paste to be hot. Roughly chop the chilies and put into blender together with all other ingredients. Blend to a smooth paste and scrape down sides of blender with a spatula. Add a little extra oil or a tablespoon of water if necessary.

*SRI LANKA*

# CEYLON CURRY PASTE

∾

1 cup (3 oz, 90g) coriander seeds

1/4 cup (3/4 oz, 21g) cumin seeds

2 teaspoons fennel seeds

2 teaspoons fenugreek seeds

2 tablespoons ground rice

2 tablespoons unsweetened, desiccated coconut

12 dried red chilies

2 cinnamon sticks, broken

2 teaspoons cardamom seeds

2 teaspoons whole cloves

2 tablespoons chopped garlic

1 tablespoon chopped fresh ginger

vinegar and water for blending

16 dried curry leaves

3 rampé, cut into 2 in (5 cm) lengths

Over medium low heat, dry roast separately the coriander, cumin, fennel and fenugreek, stirring constantly until each one smells fragrant and turns fairly dark brown. Set aside to cool. Roast ground rice and coconut until light brown and set aside to cool.

Place all roasted ingredients into electric blender container, add chilies, cinnamon, cardamom, cloves, garlic, and ginger. Blend to a smooth paste, adding a little liquid to assist movement of blades. Remove paste from container and combine with curry leaves and rampé. Store in a screw-top glass jar in refrigerator.

Use 2 tablespoons paste to every 1 lb (500 g) of meat or poultry. Proceed as for Curry Paste for Poultry (see page 16).

INDIA

# MADRAS CURRY POWDER

∽

1 cup (3 oz, 90g) coriander seeds
$^1/_2$ cup ($1^1/_2$ oz, 45g) cumin seeds
$^1/_4$ cup ($^3/_4$ oz, 21g) fennel seeds
$^1/_4$ cup ($^2/_3$ oz, 20g) black mustard seeds
$^1/_4$ cup (1/3 oz, 10g) dried red chilies (broken)
2 tablespoons whole black peppercorns
2 teaspoons fenugreek seeds
1 tablespoon ground turmeric
20 dried curry leaves

In a dry pan roast separately all ingredients, except the turmeric and curry leaves, until they smell fragrant. Grind all ingredients to a fine powder in an electric blender. Mix in ground turmeric, bottle and store in freezer or other cool, dry place.

*Note:* Use 1–2 tablespoons of powder to each 1 lb (500 g) of main ingredient.

SRI LANKA

# FRAGRANT SPICE POWDER

∽

2 teaspoons whole cloves
1 tablespoon cardamom seeds
1 tablespoon whole black peppercorns
2 tablespoons broken cinnamon stick
4 tablespoons cumin seeds

Roast these spices for 5 minutes in a dry pan over medium heat. Cool slightly and grind to a very fine consistency in an electric blender on high speed. Sprinkle a teaspoon of this powder over game or meat curries just before serving. Bottle and store away from heat and sunlight.

INDIA

# GREEN MASALA PASTE

∽

*A SPICE PASTE BASED ON CILANTRO (FRESH CORIANDER LEAVES), MINT, GARLIC, AND GINGER. ADDED TO ANY CURRY OR SPECIAL PREPARATION, IT WILL GIVE EXTRA FLAVOR. IT DOES NOT TAKE THE PLACE OF CURRY PASTE OR INDIVIDUAL SPICES.*

1 teaspoon fenugreek seeds
5 large cloves garlic
2 tablespoons finely chopped fresh ginger
1 cup ($1^1/_2$ oz, 45g) firmly packed fresh mint leaves
1 cup ($1^1/_2$ oz, 45g) firmly packed cilantro
(fresh coriander leaves)
$^1/_2$ cup (4 fl oz, 125 ml) vinegar
3 teaspoons salt
2 teaspoons ground turmeric
$^1/_2$ teaspoon ground cloves
1 teaspoon ground cardamom
$^1/_2$ cup (4 fl oz, 125ml) vegetable oil
$^1/_4$ cup (2 fl oz, 60 ml) sesame oil

Put fenugreek seeds in water to soak overnight. They will swell and develop a jelly-like coating. Measure 1 teaspoon of soaked seeds and put into container of electric blender with garlic, ginger, mint, coriander, and vinegar. Blend on high speed until very smooth. Mix in salt and ground spices.

Heat oils until very hot, add blended mixture, bring to a boil, turn off heat. Cool and bottle. Oil should cover the top of the herbs. If there is not quite enough oil, heat a little more and add it to the bottle.

See picture opposite page 19.

*MALAYSIA*

# CURRY PASTE FOR BEEF OR PORK

∾

$^3/_4$ cup ($2^1/_4$ oz, 65 g) coriander seeds

2 tablespoons cumin seeds

$^1/_4$ cup ($^1/_3$ oz, 10 g) dried red chilies, broken

2 teaspoons ground turmeric

5 candlenuts or 4 Brazil kernels, chopped

1 teaspoon laos powder

6 teaspoons chopped garlic

3 teaspoons chopped fresh ginger

4 stems fresh lemon grass, chopped or rind
of one lemon

1 tablespoon black peppercorns

3 teaspoons salt

vinegar and water for blending

Place all ingredients in an electric blender. Add a little liquid to facilitate movement of the blades and blend to a smooth paste. Allow to cool and store in a screw-top glass jar in refrigerator.

Allow 2 tablespoons of paste to every 1 lb (500 g) meat. Proceed as for Curry Paste for Poultry (see page 16).

*MALAYSIA*

# CURRY PASTE FOR FISH & SHELLFISH

∾

$^1/_2$ cup ($1^1/_2$ oz, 45 g) coriander seeds

1 tablespoon cumin seeds

2 teaspoons fennel seeds

$^1/_4$ cup ($^1/_3$ oz, 10 g) dried chilies, broken

6 teaspoons chopped garlic

4 teaspoons chopped fresh ginger

5 candlenuts or 4 Brazil kernels, chopped

1 teaspoon kencur (galangal, lesser)

2 tablespoons unsweetened desiccated coconut

3 teaspoons blachan (dried shrimp paste)

2 teaspoons tamarind paste

1 teaspoon laos powder

3 teaspoons salt

2 teaspoons ground turmeric

4 stems fresh lemon grass, chopped or rind
of 1 lemon

water for blending

Place all ingredients an electric blender. Add a little water to facilitate movement of the blades, and blend to a smooth paste. Allow to cool and store in a screw-top glass jar in refrigerator.

Allow 2 tablespoons of paste to every 1 lb (500 g) seafood. Proceed as for Curry Paste for Poultry (see recipe overleaf).

*MALAYSIA*

# CURRY PASTE FOR POULTRY

∾

$1/2$ cup ($1^1/2$ oz, 45 g) coriander seeds

1 tablespoon cumin seeds

2 teaspoons sweet cumin seeds

$1/4$ cup ($1/3$ oz, 10 g) dried red chilies, broken

5 candlenuts or 4 Brazil kernels, chopped

3 stems fresh lemon grass, finely sliced or
rind of 1 lemon

4 teaspoons chopped garlic

4 teaspoons chopped fresh ginger

2 teaspoons laos powder

3 teaspoons salt water for blending

Place all ingredients in container of electric blender. Add a little water to facilitate movement of the blades, and blend to a smooth paste. Allow to cool and store in a screw-top glass jar in refrigerator.

Allow 1–2 tablespoons paste to every 1 lb (500 g) poultry. Slice one onion and fry till soft and brown, then add paste. Fry till mixture smells fragrant and oil comes to the surface. Stir in $1/2$ cup (4 fl oz, 125 ml) hot water, cover and simmer for 10 minutes. Add poultry pieces, stir in well and simmer covered till meat is tender. Serve with boiled rice.

*THAILAND*

# RED CURRY PASTE

∾

4–6 dried red chilies

2 small brown onions, chopped

1 teaspoon black peppercorns

2 teaspoons ground cumin

1 tablespoon ground coriander

2 tablespoons chopped fresh coriander root

1 teaspoon salt

2 teaspoons chopped lemon rind

1 teaspoon serai (lemon grass) powder

1 teaspoon laos powder

1 tablespoon chopped garlic

2 teaspoons dried shrimp paste

1 tablespoon oil

1 teaspoon turmeric

2 teaspoons paprika

Remove stems from chilies, but keep the seeds in if you want the curry paste to be as hot as it is in Thailand. Break the chilies into pieces and put into container of an electric blender together with all the other ingredients. Blend to a smooth paste, stopping motor frequently and pushing ingredients onto blades. It may be necessary to add a tablespoon of water or extra oil.

*THAILAND*

# MOSLEM CURRY PASTE

∾

*YOU CAN MAKE THIS CURRY PASTE TWO WAYS — EITHER USING THE WHOLE SPICES, ROASTING AND GRINDING THEM (YOU WILL NEED A STOUT MORTAR AND PESTLE FOR THIS) OR BY USING THE GROUND SPICES. SINCE, IN SOME AREAS IT IS EASIER TO BUY WHOLE SPICES THAN IN OTHERS WHERE ONE CAN ONLY OBTAIN GROUND SPICES, I HAVE TESTED THIS RECIPE USING BOTH FORMS. ONE IS JUST AS SUCCESSFUL AS THE OTHER, AND THE GROUND SPICES CERTAINLY REQUIRE LESS EFFORT.*

7-10 dried chilies or 2 teaspoons chili powder

2 tablespoons coriander seeds or ground coriander

1 teaspoon cumin or fennel seeds or ground fennel

2 teaspoons laos powder, optional

1 teaspoon shredded lemon grass or finely peeled lemon rind

5 whole cloves or $^1/_4$ teaspoon ground cloves

1 stick cinnamon or 1 teaspoon ground cinnamon

5 cardamom pods or $^1/_2$ teaspoon ground cardamom

1 blade mace or $^1/_2$ teaspoon ground mace

2 tablespoons oil

2 medium size onions, finely sliced

$2^1/_2$ teaspoons finely chopped garlic

$^1/_2$ teaspoon dried shrimp paste

Break the chilies, shake out the seeds, and roast them lightly in a dry pan. Pound in a mortar and pestle. Roast the coriander seeds until aromatic and dark brown, shaking pan frequently or stirring. Pound in a mortar until seeds are reduced to fine powder (if spices are pounded while hot, they are easily pulverized). Roast cumin seeds until they crackle and start to pop, then grind to a powder. I have not suggested grinding them in a blender because the quantities are so small there is not enough for the blades to work on.

If using ground spices, dry-roast the ground coriander and fennel over low heat, stirring constantly and taking care they do not burn. Roast until they turn a rich brown and have an aromatic smell. It is not necessary to roast the chili powder or spices.

Add laos and lemon rind to the ground spices. Parch the cloves, cinnamon stick, cardamom pods, and mace in a dry pan over low heat, shaking the pan. Separate the cinnamon into layers, it will roast more quickly. Grind all the spices in mortar and pestle to a fine powder and combine with the previously roasted and ground ingredients. Set aside.

Heat oil in a frying pan and on low heat fry sliced onions and garlic until soft and golden brown, stirring occasionally. Add dried shrimp paste and fry for a minute longer, crushing it in the oil with back of spoon. Put this fried mixture, when it has cooled slightly, into container of electric blender with lemon rind and blend to a paste. If necessary, add a little coconut cream or water to assist action of blender. Turn into a bowl and combine with dry ground spices. The curry paste is now ready to use.

If a blender is not available, crush the onions and garlic as much as posslble after they are cooked, combine with the spices and use in the same way.

# BURMESE CURRIES

THE INGREDIENTS BASIC to all Burmese curries never vary – onion, garlic, ginger, chili, and turmeric. The chili can be used in powder form, or whole dried chilies can be ground with the other ingredients, but chili is used sparingly and may be omitted if a hot curry is not desired. There will still be lots of flavor.

The more onions used, the thicker the "gravy". To make a curry for four people using $^1/_2$ lb (750 g) of meat, fish, or poultry, here is a well-balanced mixture:

1 large onion
2 or 3 cloves of garlic
1 teaspoon finely grated fresh ginger
$^1/_2$ teaspoon ground turmeric
$^1/_4$ teaspoon chili powder
2 or 3 tablespoons oil for frying.

Light sesame oil is best for capturing the true Burmese flavor (animal fat of any sort is never used). If corn, peanut, sunflower, or other vegetable oil is used, add a small amount of Chinese-style dark sesame oil for flavor in the proportions of a teaspoon of sesame oil to a tablespoon of vegetable oil.

## Preparation of Basic Ingredients

There is only one way to cook these basic ingredients in order to achieve a mellow flavor in which no single ingredient predominates.

Grind to a purée the onion, garlic, and ginger. In the absence of the Asian grinding stone, this is best done in an electric blender, first chopping the ingredients roughly. It will be necessary to stop the motor frequently and scrape down the sides of the blender container. Or, if using the smaller blender jars (a supplement to many machines), lift off and shake the jar to redistribute the contents. When puréed smoothly, mix in the turmeric and chili powder.

Heat 3 tablespoons of oil in a saucepan until smoking hot. Be careful when putting in the ground ingredients, for the hot oil splutters violently. Reduce heat and stir well to mix ingredients with the oil. Cover pan and simmer the mixture, lifting lid frequently to stir and scrape the base of pan with a wooden spoon. This initial frying takes at least 15 minutes. If mixture fries too rapidly and begins to stick before the smell has mellowed and the onions become transparent, add a small quantity of water from time to time and stir well. When the water content of the onions has evaporated and the ingredients turn a rich red-brown color with oil showing around the edges of the mass, the first stage of cooking, and the most important one, is complete.

There is a Burmese term to describe this – see byan – meaning "oil returned", that is, with the water completely evaporated and the oil returned to just oil. The basic ingredients will not have the required flavor unless this procedure is followed. The meat, fish, or vegetables added will release their own juices while cooking slowly in the pan with the lid on. A roasting chicken will be sufficiently cooked by the time its own juices have evaporated. Boiling fowls, duck, some cuts of beef and pork may need a little water added from time to time as cooking continues until they are tender. Fish and prawns cook very quickly but some types may need a little more liquid added – fish stock, water, or coconut cream (milk). Vegetables seldom require any added liquid, but if a wetter result is preferred add water or coconut cream.

*Thai Fried Rice (page 24).*

*Ingredients for Green Masala Paste (page 14).*

# RICE, BREAD AND NOODLES

IN ANY COUNTRY where curries are eaten daily, you will find that rice or noodles or many varieties of bread form the main part of the diet.

So great are the varieties of bread, and ways of cooking rice, that these recipes are only a sampling of a subject that could fill a book on its own. However, included in this section are recipes that are representative of each of the curry-eating countries.

Three or four times as much rice or bread should be eaten with the curried meat, fish or poultry. In this way no digestive problems will be experienced. For the Westerner this a different but essential concept to grasp, when they have been used to considering meat, fish or poultry the main part of the meal.

While rice cooked in coconut cream or spicy stock is very nice for special occasions, perfectly cooked plain white rice or unpolished rice is served most often and really best combines with curries. Learn to cook rice by the absorption method as outlined in the recipes that follow. You will soon appreciate why so many millions in Asia think of rice as the most important food item and why, when asking if you have dined, the question, literally translated is: "Have you eaten rice?"

*THROUGHOUT ASIA*

# STEAMED RICE

∾

*THERE ARE AS MANY WAYS OF COOKING RICE AS THERE ARE COOKS. SOME WASH THE RICE SEVERAL TIMES, OTHERS BELIEVE THAT VALUABLE NUTRIENTS ARE LOST IN WASHING. USE YOUR DISCRETION — SOME IMPORTED RICE REALLY NEEDS WASHING — BUT DRAIN IT WELL SO THE PROPORTION OF WATER TO RICE IS RETAINED. CHARMAINE.*

SERVES: 6

500 g (1 lb) long grain rice
4 cups (32 fl oz, 1 l) water
$2^1/_2$ teaspoons salt, optional

Use a saucepan with a well fitting lid. If using a stainless steel pan of the type where the lid forms a seal, reduce water by $^1/_4$ cup (2 fl oz, 60 ml).

Put rice, water, and salt into pan and bring to a boil. As soon as it comes to a boil turn heat very low, cover tightly and allow to cook for 20 minutes. The liquid should be completely absorbed and the rice cooked perfectly. Uncover and allow steam to escape for a few minutes, then fluff rice with a fork and serve up using a metal spoon, for a wooden spoon would crush the grains.

Short Grain Rice: If cooking short grain rice, remember that the absorption rate is not as great as that of long grain rice. For 1 lb (500 g) rice, allow $2^1/_2$ cups (20 fl oz, 600 ml) water for a very firm result, or 3 cups (24 fl oz, 750 ml) water for rice that is slightly softer but with each grain separate and not mushy.

Unpolished or Natural Rice: Rice that has not had its outer layer of bran removed is more nutritious as it is rich in Vitamin B. It does, however, take longer to cook. Use the same measurement as for long grain rice, or if a more tender result is preferred, add an extra $^1/_2$ cup (4 fl oz, 125 ml) water. Cook in the same way, on very low heat, for 40 to 45 minutes.

*Note:* A most important point when cooking rice is that the lid should not be lifted during cooking time, for steam is lost and can affect the cooking time and the final result. Also, rice is never stirred during cooking. If rice needs washing, allow to drain in colander before starting to cook, or the measurement of water will not be accurate. Some cooks prefer to bring the water to a boil and then add the rice, but I find that either way the results are perfect as long as the measurements of rice and water are accurate and the rules for gentle steaming in a tightly covered pan are observed.

*INDIA*

# STEAMED RICE

∾

SERVES: 6

$2^1/_2$ cups (20 oz, 600 ml) long grain rice
2 teaspoons ghee
4 cups (32 fl oz, 1 L) hot water
$2^1/_2$ teaspoons salt, optional

Wash rice well if necessary. Drain in colander for 30 minutes. Heat ghee in a heavy-based saucepan with a well-fitting lid. Add rice and fry, stirring for about 2 minutes. Add hot water and salt, stir and bring quickly to the boil. Turn heat very low, cover tightly and cook, without lifting lid or stirring, for 20 to 25 minutes. Uncover to allow steam to escape for a minute or two, then lightly fluff up rice with fork, taking care not to mash the grains, which will be firm and separate and perfectly cooked. Dish up using a slotted metal spoon rather than a wooden spoon which will crush the grains. Serve with curries or other spiced dishes.

SRI LANKA

# YELLOW RICE
∾

*THIS IS SO RICH AND FULL OF FLAVOR THAT IT IS SERVED ONLY ON SPECIAL OCCASIONS. REUBEN.*

SERVES: 6

1 lb (500 g) long grain rice
4 tablespoons ghee
2 medium onions, finely sliced
6 cloves
20 black peppercorns
12 cardamom pods, bruised
1$^1/_2$ teaspoons ground turmeric
3$^1/_2$ teaspoons salt
12 curry leaves
1 stem lemon grass, optional
4 pieces daun pandan or rampé leaf, optional
about 4 cups (32 fl oz) coconut cream

Wash rice and drain thoroughly. Heat ghee in a large saucepan, add onion and fry until it begins to turn golden brown. Add cloves, peppercorns, cardamom pods, turmeric, salt, curry leaves, lemon grass, and pandan or rampé leaf. Add rice and fry, stirring constantly, for 2 to 3 minutes, until rice is well coated with ghee and turmeric. Add coconut cream and bring to a boil. Reduce heat, cover and cook for 20 to 25 minutes without lifting lid.

When rice is cooked, the spices will have come to the top. Remove spices and leaves used for flavoring and fluff up the rice lightly with a fork. Serve hot, with curries and accompaniments.

INDIA

# SAVORY RICE & LENTILS
∾

*A GOOD ONE-DISH MEAL AND OFTEN THE BASIS OF A VEGETARIAN MENU AS THE LENTILS PROVIDE PROTEIN. CHARMAINE.*

SERVES: 4-6

1 cup (8 oz, 250 g) long grain rice
1 cup (6 oz, 185 g) red lentils
2$^1/_2$ tablespoons ghee
2 medium onions, finely sliced
3$^1/_2$ cups (28 fl oz, 875 ml) hot water
2$^1/_2$ teaspoons salt
1$^1/_2$ teaspoons garam masala (see page 12)

Wash rice and drain well. Wash lentils well, removing any that float to the surface, then drain thoroughly.

Heat ghee in a saucepan and fry onion gently until golden brown. Remove half the onion and reserve. Add rice and lentils to pan and fry, stirring constantly for about 3 minutes. Add hot water, salt, and garam masala. Bring to a boil, cover and simmer over very low heat for 20 to 25 minutes or until rice and lentils are cooked. Do not lift the lid or stir during cooking time. Serve hot, garnished with reserved fried onion, and accompanied by curries.

*Note:* Whole spices, e.g. small cinnamon stick and a few whole cloves, cardamoms, and peppercorns may be used instead of garam masala.

*BURMA*

# RICE NOODLES WITH CURRY

∽

*THIS BURMESE CURRY IS ALMOST LIKE A SOUP AND MAKES A SIMPLE, DELICIOUS MEAL. CHARMAINE.*

SERVES: 6–8

1 x 3 lb (1.5 kg) roasting chicken
1 teaspoon ground turmeric
2 teaspoons salt
$^1/_4$ cup (2 fl oz, 60 ml) fish sauce (see Glossary)
$1^1/_2$ cups (12 fl oz, 375 ml) thick coconut cream 3 large onions, finely sliced
$1^1/_2$ teaspoons finely chopped garlic
$^1/_2$ cup (4 oz, 125 ml) besan (chickpea flour)
2 cups (16 fl oz, 500 ml) thin coconut cream
4 eggs, hard-cooked (boiled)
1 lb (500 g) rice noodles, dried or 2 lb (1 kg) fresh rice noodles
2 teaspoons chili oil (see Glossary)

Joint chicken and put into a saucepan with turmeric, salt, fish sauce, and just enough water to almost cover. Bring to a boil then reduce heat, cover and simmer until chicken is tender. Cool, then discard bones and cut meat into small pieces.

Cook thick coconut cream in a saucepan, stirring constantly, until it becomes thick and oil rises to the top. Keep cooking until it is very oily, then add the onions and garlic and fry, stirring, until they start to color.

Add chicken to the frying onions and cook, stirring constantly for a few minutes. Set aside.

Mix besan with cold water to form a thin cream. Add thin coconut cream to the pan and when it comes to a boil stir in the besan mixture. Cook and stir constantly until it thickens, taking care it does not become lumpy or catch to the base of the pan. Add strained chicken stock a little at a time until the gravy is as thick as that of a stew. Add the chicken and onion mixture.

cut them into narrow strips and pour boiling water over them in a colander or steam gently for a few minutes to heat through. Bring the chicken combination to simmering point, stir in chili oil and remove from the heat. Serve in a large bowl, with noodles, sliced hard-cooked eggs, and raw onions served separately.

*MALAYSIA*

# COCONUT RICE

∽

SERVES: 4–5

1 lb (500 g) medium or long grain rice
$1^1/_4$ cups (10 fl oz, 300 ml) coconut cream $2^1/_2$ teaspoons salt

Soak rice in cold water overnight. Drain rice, spread in top part of a steamer and steam over rapidly boiling water for 30 minutes. Halfway through steaming, stir rice and turn it so that the rice on the bottom comes to the top and vice versa.

Gently heat the coconut cream with the salt in a large saucepan, stirring. Do not boil. Add the steamed rice, stir well, cover tightly and let stand for a further 30 minutes, by which time the cream should be completely absorbed. Once more spread the rice in top of steamer, bring water back to a boil and steam for 30 minutes, starting on high heat and gradually turning heat lower until in the end the water merely simmers. Serve hot with meat, poultry, fish, or vegetable dishes.

If fresh rice noodles are bought as large sheets,

SRI LANKA

# GHEE RICE

∾

*VERY RICH, VERY SPICY, VERY, VERY TASTY. REUBEN.*

SERVES: 4–5

> 1 lb (500 g ) basmati or other long grain rice
> 2¹/₂ tablespoons ghee
> 1 large onion, finely sliced
> 4 whole cloves
> 6 cardamom pods, bruised
> 1 cinnamon stick
> 4 cups (32 fl oz, 1 l) beef, chicken, or mutton stock,
> or water and stock cubes
> 2¹/₂ teaspoons salt

Wash rice well and drain for at least 30 minutes. Heat ghee in a saucepan and fry onion until golden, add spices and drained rice. Fry, stirring with slotted metal spoon, for 5 minutes over a moderate heat. Add hot stock and salt and bring to a boil.

Reduce heat to very low, cover pan tightly with lid and cook for 15 to 20 minutes without lifting lid. At end of cooking time, uncover and allow steam to escape for 5 minutes. Gently fluff up rice with a fork, removing whole spices.

When transferring rice to a serving dish, again use a slotted metal spoon to avoid crushing grains of rice. Serve hot, accompanied by curries of meat and vegetables, pickles, and sambols.

MALAYSIA

# GLUTINOUS YELLOW RICE

∾

*DON'T EXPECT THIS RICE TO BE LIGHT AND FLUFFY — THE STICKY CONSISTENCY IS HOW MALAYSIANS LIKE IT. CHARMAINE.*

SERVES: 6

> 1 lb (500 g) glutinous rice
> 2 cups (16 fl oz, 500 ml) water
> 2 teaspoons salt
> 1 clove garlic, crushed
> 1 teaspoon ground turmeric
> ¹/₂ teaspoon ground black pepper
> 1 daun pandan
> 2 cups (16 fl oz, 500 ml) hot coconut cream
> (see page 8)

> GARNISH:
> crisp fried onion flakes

Wash rice and drain. Put into a saucepan with water, salt, garlic, turmeric, pepper and pandanus leaf for flavoring. Bring to a boil, reduce heat, cover tightly and steam for 10 minutes.

Uncover, add coconut cream (which should be very hot), and with a long-pronged fork stir gently so that the rice is mixed with the coconut cream. Cover and cook 10 minutes longer. Serve garnished with onion flakes and accompanied by curries and other dishes.

*THAILAND*

# THAI FRIED RICE

∾

*SERVE THIS BY ITSELF AS A SNACK, OR WITH CURRY AS A MEAL.*
*CHARMAINE.*

SERVES: 4

4 cups (1$^1/_2$ lb, 750 g) cold cooked rice
3 tablespoons peanut oil
2 medium onions, finely chopped
1 large pork chop, finely diced
8 oz (250 g) raw shrimp (prawns), shelled and
deveined
6 oz (185 g) crab meat
3 eggs, beaten
salt and pepper to taste
2 tablespoons fish sauce (see Glossary)
1 tablespoon chili sauce, optional
2 tablespoons tomato paste
1 cup (4 oz, 125 g) chopped scallions (spring onions)
3 tablespoons chopped cilantro (fresh coriander leaves)

Cook rice, spread out and allow to cool. Heat oil
in a wok or large frying pan and fry the onions
on medium low heat, stirring constantly, until
soft and translucent. Increase heat to high. Add
pork and fry for 3 minutes. Add shrimps and crab
meat and fry for a further 3 minutes or until
cooked.

Season beaten eggs well with salt and pepper
and pour into middle of wok. Stir until just
beginning to set, then add rice and stir well.
Continue tossing and stirring until rice is heated
through. Sprinkle fish sauce over and mix well,
then add chili sauce and tomato paste and toss
thoroughly so the rice has a reddish color.
Remove from heat, stir the scallions through, and
transfer to serving platter. Sprinkle with chopped
cilantro and serve.

See picture opposite page 18.

*INDONESIA*

# RICE COOKED IN COCONUT CREAM WITH SPICES

∾

SERVES: 6

1 lb (500 g) long grain rice
4$^1/_2$ cups (36 fl oz, 1.25 l) coconut cream
2$^1/_2$ teaspoons salt
1 onion, finely chopped
1 teaspoon finely chopped garlic
1 teaspoon ground turmeric
1 teaspoon ground cumin
2 teaspoons ground coriander
$^1/_2$ teaspoon dried shrimp paste
$^1/_4$ teaspoon kencur (galangal, lesser) powder
1 teaspoon finely chopped lemon rind,
or 1 stem of lemon grass, chopped

If rice needs washing, wash and drain well. Put
all ingredients except rice into a saucepan with a
well fitting lid, and bring slowly to a boil, uncovered, stirring frequently.

Add the rice, stir and bring back to a boil.
Turn heat as low as possible, cover pan tightly
and steam for 20 minutes. Uncover, fork rice
lightly from around sides of pan, mixing in any
coconut cream that has not been absorbed,
replace lid and steam for 5 minutes longer. Serve
hot with Indonesian or Malaysian curries and
accompaniments.

*INDIA*

# RICE COOKED IN STOCK WITH SPICES

~

*THIS CLASSIC PILAU GOES BEST WITH NORTH INDIAN CURRIES LIKE LAMB KORMA OR HUNDRED ALMOND CURRY. CHARMAINE.*

SERVES: 4–6

2 lb (1 kg) chicken or 3 lamb shanks
4 cardamom pods
10 whole black peppercorns
4$^1/_2$ teaspoons salt
1 onion
3 whole cloves
2$^1/_2$ cups (20 oz, 330 g) long grain rice
5 tablespoons ghee
1 large onion, finely sliced
$^1/_4$ teaspoon saffron strands or $^1/_8$ teaspoon powdered saffron
2 cloves garlic, crushed
$^1/_2$ teaspoon finely grated fresh ginger
$^1/_2$ teaspoon garam masala (see page 12)
$^1/_2$ teaspoon ground cardamom
3 tablespoons rose water
$^1/_4$ cup (1$^1/_2$ oz, 45 g) sultanas

GARNISH:
$^1/_4$ cup (1 oz, 30 g) fried almonds
1 cup (6 oz, 185 g) hot cooked green peas
3 hard-cooked (boiled) eggs, halved

Make a strong, well-flavored stock by simmering chicken or lamb in water to cover, with cardamom pods, peppercorns, 2 teaspoons salt, and the onion stuck with cloves. Simmer for approximately 2 hours. Cool slightly, strain stock and measure 4 cups (32 fl oz, 1 L). Remove meat from bones, cut into bite-size pieces and set aside.

Wash rice thoroughly in water, drain in a colander and allow to dry for at least 1 hour. Heat ghee in a large saucepan and fry sliced onion until golden. Add the saffron, garlic, and ginger and fry for 1 minute, stirring constantly. Add rice and fry 5 minutes longer over a moderate heat, stirring with a slotted metal spoon.

(This prevents breaking the long delicate grains of rice which add so much to the appearance of this dish.) Add hot stock, garam masala, cardamom, remaining salt, rose water, sultanas, and reserved chicken pieces, and stir well. Cover pan with a tightly fitting lid and cook over a very low heat for 20 minutes. Do not uncover saucepan or stir rice during cooking time.

When rice is cooked, remove from heat, and leave uncovered for 5 minutes. Fluff up rice gently with a fork and place in a dish, again using a slotted metal spoon. Garnish with almonds, peas, and eggs and serve hot accompanied by an Indian curry, pickles, sliced cucumbers in sour cream or yoghurt, and crisp fried pappadams.

# OIL RICE

∾

SERVES: 4–6

2 cups (16 oz, 500 ml) glutinous rice
3 large onions
1 1/2 teaspoons turmeric
6 tablespoons oil
4 cups (32 fl oz, 1 L) hot water
2 teaspoons salt
4 tablespoons toasted sesame seeds

Wash rice well and leave to drain and dry. Slice onions thinly, keeping them uniform in thickness. Sprinkle turmeric over onions and mix lightly. Heat oil in a medium-size saucepan and fry onions until brown. Remove two-thirds of the onions and set aside for garnish. Add rice to pan and stir until it is well mixed with the oil. Add water and salt, stir well and bring to a boil. Turn heat very low, cover tightly and cook for 20 minutes by which time the rice should be cooked and the water completely absorbed.

Serve hot, garnished with fried onion and accompanied by the sesame seed lightly bruised and mixed with a little salt.

*Note:* Some people like a crust on the rice. To encourage a crust to form leave the rice on low heat for 5 to 10 minutes longer until a slight crackling sound is heard.

# CHAPATIS

∾

*FLAT DISCS OF UNLEAVENED BREAD, WITH A DELIGHTFUL FLAVOR AND CHEWY TEXTURE. SERVE WITH THE DRY TYPE OF CURRIES WHICH CAN BE SCOOPED UP ON A PIECE OF CHAPATI. CHARMAINE.*

YIELD: 20–24

3 cups (12 oz, 375 g) fine wholewheat (wholemeal) flour or roti flour (see Glossary)
1–1 1/2 teaspoons salt, or to taste
1 tablespoon ghee or oil, optional
1 cup (8 fl oz, 250 ml) lukewarm water

Put flour in mixing bowl, reserving about 1/2 cup (2oz, 60 g) for rolling chapatis. Mix salt through the flour in the bowl, then rub in ghee or oil, if used. Add water all at once and mix to a firm but not stiff dough. Knead dough for at least 10 minutes (the more it is kneaded, the lighter the bread will be). Form dough into a ball, cover with clear plastic wrap (film) and stand for 1 hour or longer. (If left overnight the chapatis will be very light and tender.)

Shape dough into balls about the size of a large walnut. Roll out each one on a lightly floured board (using reserved flour) to a circular shape as thin as a French crêpe. After rolling out chapatis, heat a griddle plate or heavy-based frying pan until very hot, and cook the chapatis, starting with those that were rolled first (the resting between rolling and cooking seems to make for lighter chapatis). Put chapati on griddle and leave for about 1 minute. Turn and cook other side a further minute, pressing lightly around the edges of the chapati with a folded tea cloth (towel) or an egg slice. This encourages bubbles to form and makes the chapatis light. As each one is cooked, wrap in a clean tea cloth until all are ready. Serve immediately with butter, dry curries, or vegetable dishes.

*Note:* In India, the chapatis are cooked on the tawa or griddle and are held for a moment or two right over the fire. This makes them puff up like balloons. You can do this over a gas flame, holding them with kitchen tongs.

See picture opposite page 99.

*INDIA*

# PARATHA

### *Flaky Wholewheat (Wholemeal) Bread*

∾

*THIS WOULD HAVE TO BE MY FAVORITE AMONG THE INDIAN
BREADS AND MY THANKS GO TO AN OLD FAMILY FRIEND WHO
TAUGHT ME THIS VERY EASY METHOD OF ACHIEVING THE
NUMEROUS FLAKY LAYERS THAT MAKE PARATHAS SO SPECIAL.
CHARMAINE.*

MAKES: 12–14

1¹/₂ cups (6 oz, 185 g) fine wholemeal flour
1¹/₂ cups (6 oz, 185 g) all purpose (plain white)
flour or roti flour (see Glossary)
1¹/₂ teaspoons salt
6-8 tablespoons ghee
1 cup (8 fl oz, 250 ml) water
extra ghee for cooking

Sieve wholewheat flour, all purpose flour and salt
into a mixing bowl and rub in 1 tablespoon of the
ghee. Add water, mix and knead dough as for
chapatis. Cover dough with clear plastic and set
aside for 1 hour.

Divide dough into 12–14 equal portions and
roll each into a smooth ball. Melt ghee over a low
heat and cool slightly. Roll each ball of dough on
a lightly floured board into a very thin circular
shape. Pour about 2 teaspoons of the melted ghee
into the middle of each and spread lightly with
the hand.

With a knife, make a cut from the middle of
each circle to the outer edge. Starting at the cut
edge, roll the dough closely into a cone shape.
Pick it up, press the apex of the cone and the
base towards each other and flatten slightly. You
will now have a small, roughly circular lump of
dough again. Lightly flour the board again and roll
out the dough very gently, taking care not to
press too hard so that the air does not escape at
the edges. The parathas should be as round as
possible, but not as thinly rolled as the first time
– about the size of a breakfast plate.

See picture opposite page 99.

Cook on a hot griddle liberally greased with
extra ghee, turning parathas and spreading with
more ghee, until they are golden brown. Serve
hot with curries or grilled kebabs, sambals and
fresh mint chutney (see page 89).

*Note*: The wholewheat and all purpose or roti
flour can be replaced by 3 cups (12 oz, 375 g) all
purpose flour.

*INDIA*

# PURI

### *Deep-fried Wholewheat (Wholemeal) Bread*

∾

*CHILDREN LOVE THIS CRISP, WHOLEWHEAT BREAD. CHARMAINE.*

Proceed as for chapatis. When all the dough is
rolled out heat approximately 1 in (2.5 cm) of oil
in a deep frying pan. When a faint haze rises from
the oil, fry puris one at a time, over a moderate
heat. Spoon hot oil continually over the cooking
puri until it puffs and swells. Turn over and fry
other side in the same way. When both sides are
pale golden brown, drain on absorbent paper.
Serve immediately with curries.

See picture opposite page 99.

*Note*: Puri is pronounced "poo-ree".

# MEAT

PORK IS WIDELY used in Asia, for pigs are the cheapest animals to raise. Sheep and goats are used for mutton, and beef may come from buffaloes more often than from bulls.

While tender lamb, beef, or pork is desirable for quickly cooked dishes like satays, kebabs, and so on, for curries it is actually an advantage to use the cuts of meat which allow for longer cooking.

The longer and more slowly a curry is cooked, the more the flavors blend and mellow. If prepared a day or two (or even more) ahead of time, they actually improve. And each reheating seems to make the curry taste better. Here is the best solution for using more economical cuts – curry them! An added bonus is that the economy meats like skirt or flank steak, shin or gravy beef, hogget, pork belly and so on, are more tasty than tender fillet and are therefore the best choice for cooking with robust spices. Your venture into curry cookery may also be a means of lowering the food budget.

Do remember, when cooking beef or mutton, to trim off all excess fat. Even pork, though essentially a fatty meat, should not be too fat if a meal is to be appreciated and not followed by that "too rich" feeling which is so unwelcome. Always serve meat curries with a large proportion of rice or bread to offset the spiciness and absorb the richness.

Although to the average westerner, meat is the main part of the meal, prepared as curry it cannot be eaten in so large a quantity. There should be at least twice as much rice or bread to help it down. For a world that is looking at ways to reduce the consumption of meat, both for economic and health reasons, this may well be the solution!

SRI LANKA

# BEEF SMOORE

∾

*POT ROAST GLORIFIED. AND HOW! REUBEN.*

SERVES: 6–8

3 lb (1.5 kg) fresh silverside or other stewing steak,
in one piece
2 medium onions, finely chopped
3 teaspoons finely chopped garlic
1 tablespoon finely chopped fresh ginger
1 stick cinnamon
10 curry leaves
1 stem fresh lemon grass or 2 strips lemon rind
3 tablespoons Ceylon curry powder (see page 12)
$^1/_2$ teaspoon fenugreek seeds
$^1/_2$ cup (4 fl oz, 125 ml) vinegar
$^1/_2$ pickled lime or lemon or $^1/_2$ cup tamarind liquid
(see Glossary)
2 cups (16 fl oz, 500 ml) thin coconut cream
1 teaspoon ground turmeric
2 teaspoons chili powder, or to taste
2 teaspoons salt, or to taste
1 cup (8 fl oz, 250 ml) thick coconut cream
$2^1/_2$ tablespoons ghee

Pierce the meat well with a skewer and put in a large saucepan with all the ingredients except the thick coconut cream and ghee. Cover and simmer gently until meat is tender, approximately $1^1/_2$ to 2 hours. Add thick coconut cream and cook, uncovered for 15 minutes longer.

Lift meat out on to a serving dish and if gravy is too thin, reduce by boiling rapidly uncovered. Transfer gravy to a bowl. Rinse pan to remove any gravy, return to stove and heat ghee in it. Fry meat on all sides, pour gravy over meat and heat through.

To serve, cut meat into thick slices and spoon gravy over.

See picture opposite page 34.

SRI LANKA

# BEEF CURRY

∾

SERVES: 8–10

3 lb (1.5 kg) stewing beef steak
3 tablespoons ghee or oil
2 large onions, finely chopped
1 tablespoon finely chopped fresh ginger
3 teaspoons finely chopped garlic
4 tablespoons Ceylon curry powder (see page 12)
1 teaspoon ground turmeric
2 teaspoons black mustard seeds
2 teaspoons salt
1 tablespoon vinegar
2 fresh red chilies, seeded and chopped
3 ripe tomatoes, peeled and chopped

Cut steak into 2 in (5 cm) squares. Heat ghee in saucepan and gently fry onions, ginger, and garlic until just beginning to turn golden. Add curry powder, turmeric, mustard seeds and fry over low heat for 2 to 3 minutes. Add salt and vinegar and stir well. Add steak and fry, stirring to coat meat well. Add chilies and tomatoes, cover pan and simmer on very low heat for about 2 hours. Serve with rice and other accompaniments. If gravy is too thin when meat is tender, cook over high heat, uncovered, until reduced.

*THAILAND*

# RED CURRY OF BEEF

∽

*DRIED MAKRUD (CITRUS) RIND AND CITRUS LEAVES GIVE THE
DISTINCTIVE LEMONY TANG TO THIS CURRY. CHARMAINE.*

SERVES: 6

2 lb (1 kg) stewing steak
2 cups (16 fl oz, 500 ml) thick coconut cream
3 tablespoons red curry paste (see page 16)
2 cups (16 fl oz, 500 ml) thin coconut cream
2 sprigs tender citrus leaves
1 tablespoon dried makrud rind, soaked
1 teaspoon salt
2 tablespoons fish sauce (see Glossary)
2 fresh red chilies, seeded and sliced

Trim the meat and cut into cubes. Use undiluted coconut cream, checking the label first to ensure it does not contain a stabilizer. Simmer in a large saucepan, stirring constantly, until it comes to a boil, then cook over a low heat until the cream thickens and the oil starts to show around the edges. Add the curry paste and fry for 5 minutes or so, stirring constantly.

When done, the curry paste will smell fragrant and mellow, and oil will start to separate from the mass again. Add beef and stir well, then add thin coconut cream. Add all remaining ingredients. Stir while bringing to a boil, then lower heat and simmer uncovered until beef is tender. If the beef is not yet tender and the gravy seems to be cooking away, add a little more coconut cream or hot water and stir. The gravy should be rich and red, and there should be quite a lot of it. Serve with white rice and side dishes.

See picture opposite title page.

*SRI LANKA*

# BEEF PEPPER CURRY

∽

*WHEN IN COLOMBO, THIS DISH HAS PRIORITY IN MY SELECTION
OF SRI LANKAN CURRIES. REUBEN.*

SERVES: 8

2 lb (1 kg) lean stewing steak
2 teaspoons salt
2-4 teaspoons ground black pepper
1 tablespoon ground coriander
2 teaspoons ground cumin
1 teaspoon ground fennel
$1/2$ teaspoon ground turmeric
2 medium onions, finely chopped
$1^1/2$ teaspoons finely chopped garlic
$1^1/2$ teaspoons finely grated fresh ginger
2 fresh red chilies, seeded and sliced
8 curry leaves
2 strips daun pandan (rampé leaf)
1 stem fresh lemon grass or 2 strips lemon rind
2 tablespoons vinegar
2 cups (16 fl oz, 500 ml) thin coconut cream
1 tablespoon ghee or oil
1 cup (8 fl oz, 250 ml) thick coconut cream

Cut the meat into 2 in (5 cm) squares and beat lightly with a meat mallet. Season with salt and pepper and mix well. Roast separately in a dry pan the coriander, cumin, and fennel. Add coriander to meat and set aside the cumin and fennel. Put meat into a saucepan with spices and all other ingredients except roasted cumin, fennel, ghee, and the thick coconut cream.

Bring slowly to a boil, reduce heat and simmer covered, until meat is tender. If gravy thickens too quickly add a little water. Pour gravy into another pan, then add the ghee or oil to the meat left in the pan and fry it for a few minutes, stirring. Add the cumin and fennel to the thick coconut cream and mix with the cooked gravy. Return everything to pan with the meat and continue to simmer uncovered over a very low heat until the gravy is thick and the various ingredients are well blended. Serve with rice and other accompaniments.

# BEEF CURRY, VERY DRY

~

SERVES: 4–6

1¹/₂ lb (750 g) stewing steak
2 large onions
5 large cloves garlic
2 teaspoons chopped fresh ginger
1 teaspoon ground turmeric
1 teaspoon chili powder
6 tablespoons light sesame oil or corn oil
1¹/₄ teaspoon ground black pepper
2 tender stems lemon grass, finely sliced,
or 4 strips lemon rind
1 cup (8 fl oz, 250 ml) hot water
1¹/₂ teaspoons salt

### GARNISH
2 large onions, finely sliced and fried until crisp
and brown

Cut beef into 2 in (5 cm) squares. Cook basic ingredients as described on page 18. When well cooked and sizzling, add beef, pepper, and lemon grass or rind. Continue frying and stirring until all juices from the beef have completely evaporated and meat is browned.

Add water and salt, cover and simmer until meat is tender, adding more water if necessary. Remove lid, raise heat and cook rapidly until the meat is oily-dry and well coated with the gravy. Garnish with fried onions and serve with white rice and accompaniments.

# MEAT & POTATO CURRY

~

*A GOOD RECIPE WHEN WATCHING THE BUDGET. LESS MEAT, MORE POTATOES, AND STILL DELICIOUS. CHARMAINE.*

SERVES: 6–8

3 lb (1.5 kg) hogget or beef
¹/₄ cup (2 fl oz, 60 ml) oil or 2 tablespoons ghee
1 teaspoon black mustard seeds
¹/₂ teaspoon fenugreek seeds
3 teaspoons finely chopped garlic
1 tablespoon finely chopped fresh ginger
3 medium onions, finely sliced
1¹/₂ teaspoons ground turmeric
2 tablespoons ground coriander
1 tablespoon ground cumin
2 teaspoons chili powder
3 teaspoons salt
2 tablespoons vinegar
2 teaspoons garam masala (see page 12)
2 tablespoons extra vinegar
1¹/₂ lb (750 g) potatoes, peeled and cubed
2 tablespoons chopped cilantro (fresh coriander leaves)

Trim fat and gristle from meat and cut into small cubes. Heat oil in a large saucepan and fry the mustard seeds until they pop. Add fenugreek seeds, garlic, ginger, and onion and fry over medium heat, stirring occasionally with a wooden spoon, until onions just begin to brown. Add turmeric, coriander, cumin, and chili powder and stir for a minute or so. Add salt and vinegar and stir until liquid dries up. Sprinkle in the garam masala and mix well. Add the cubed meat, stirring so all pieces are coated with the spice mixture. If some of the spice begins to catch to the base of the pan, add the extra vinegar and stir, scraping as much as possible from the base of the pan.

Reduce heat, cover and simmer for 1¹/₂ to 2 hours or until meat is tender. It may be necessary to add a little water. Add the cubed potatoes, cover once more and cook for 20 to 25 minutes or until done. Sprinkle with cilantro and serve hot with rice or Indian bread.

*NORTH INDIA*

# KOFTA CURRY

∾

*YOU'LL NEVER DREAM GROUND MEAT CAN TASTE SO GOOD.*
*CHARMAINE.*

SERVES: 6

### KOFTAS:

1¹/₂ lb (750 g) finely ground lamb
1 medium onion, finely chopped
¹/₂ teaspoon crushed garlic
¹/₂ teaspoon finely grated fresh ginger
1 red or green fresh chili, seeded and finely chopped
3 tablespoons chopped cilantro (fresh coriander leaves)
or fresh mint
1¹/₂ teaspoons salt
1 teaspoon garam masala (see page 12)

### GRAVY:

3 tablespoons ghee or oil
2 medium onions, finely chopped
1 teaspoon finely chopped garlic
1 tablespoon finely chopped fresh ginger
1 teaspoon ground turmeric
1 teaspoon garam masala
1 teaspoon chili powder
2 ripe tomatoes, peeled and chopped
1 teaspoon salt
2 tablespoons chopped cilantro (fresh coriander leaves)
or mint
lemon juice to taste

*Koftas:* Mix ground lamb thoroughly with all the other ingredients. Shape into small balls.

*Gravy:* Heat ghee in a large, heavy saucepan, brown the koftas, remove from pan and set aside. In the same pan fry the onion, garlic, and ginger until soft and golden. Add turmeric, garam masala, and chili powder, fry for 1 minute. Add tomato, salt, and koftas, cover and simmer for 25 minutes or until gravy is thick and koftas tender. Stir in chopped herbs and lemon juice. Serve with rice or chapatis and various accompaniments.

*INDIA*

# BEEF & CARDAMOM CURRY

∾

*A FAIRLY STRONG FLAVOR OF CARDAMOM DISTINGUISHES*
*THIS CURRY. REUBEN.*

SERVES: 4

1 lb (500 g) lean stewing steak
2 tablespoons peanut oil
1 large onion, sliced
1 teaspoon finely chopped garlic
1 teaspoon finely chopped fresh ginger
¹/₂ teaspoon turmeric
2 teaspoons ground cardamom
1 teaspoon ground coriander
1 teaspoon ground cumin
1 x 2 in (5 cm) cinnamon stick
pinch of ground cloves
1 teaspoon chili powder
1 tablespoon lemon juice
6 curry leaves
salt to taste
¹/₂ cup (4 fl oz, 125 ml) warm water

Cut meat into 2 in (5 cm) squares. Heat oil in a saucepan, add onions and fry, stirring occasionally, until golden brown. Add meat, raise heat and brown all over. Add all other ingredients except the water, mix with the meat and cook for 3 minutes.

Add water, lower heat, cover and simmer till meat is tender, adding more water if necessary. Stir occasionally to prevent meat catching to base of saucepan. Serve with boiled rice and accompaniments.

# JAVANESE GROUND STEAK CURRY

∾

*VERY POPULAR WITH THE JUNIOR SET, AND YOU CAN LEAVE OUT THE CHILI POWDER IF YOU (OR THEY) PREFER. CHARMAINE.*

1 lb (500 g) ground (minced) steak
1 medium onion, roughly chopped
1 teaspoon chopped garlic
1 teaspoon laos powder
1 teaspoon ground coriander
1 teaspoon shrimp paste
$^1/_4$ cup (1 oz) roasted peanuts
teaspoon ground black pepper
1 teaspoon chili powder
$^1/_4$ cup (2 fl oz) warm water
1 tablespoon peanut oil
1 stem lemon grass or chopped rind of $^1/_2$ lemon
1 teaspoon salt
$^1/_4$ cup thick coconut cream

Into an electric blender put onion, garlic, laos powder, coriander, shrimp paste, peanuts, pepper and chili powder. Blend to a paste adding a little water to facilitate blending.

Heat oil in a saucepan, stir in the contents of blender, add lemon grass or lemon rind and fry for 5 minutes. Sprinkle in 1 teaspoon salt, stir, cover and simmer for 30 minutes. Add the coconut cream and cook uncovered for a further 10 minutes, stirring frequently. Serve with hot boiled rice, fried shrimp wafers or other side dishes.

# MOSLEM BEEF CURRY

∾

SERVES: 6–8

2 lb (1 kg) stewing beef
2 tablespoons peanut oil
2 teaspoons finely chopped garlic
1 large onion, sliced
2 tablespoons Moslem curry paste (see page 17)
2 tablespoons basil leaves or 2 teaspoons dried basil
1 teaspoon chili powder
2 teaspoons sugar
2 in (5 cm) cinnamon stick
2 teaspoons salt
1 cup (8 fl oz, 250 ml) warm water
4 tablespoons thick coconut cream

GARNISH:
$^1/_2$ cup (2 oz) chopped, roasted peanuts

Cut beef into 2.5 cm (1 in) squares. Heat oil in a saucepan and add garlic and sliced onion and fry till golden brown. Add meat and brown on high heat, stirring frequently.

Stir in the curry paste, basil leaves, chili powder, sugar, cinnamon and salt. Add water and bring to a boil, cover and simmer till meat is tender and oil comes to the surface. Stir in the coconut cream, simmer 2 minutes longer uncovered and serve garnished with chopped peanuts.

*MALAYSIA*

# SATAY CURRY

∾

*WHILE MEAT MARINATES, PREPARE GRAVY, OR IF MORE CONVE-
NIENT, PREPARE GRAVY A DAY OR TWO BEFORE — IT IMPROVES
THE FLAVOR. BROIL (GRILL) SATAYS JUST BEFORE SERVING.*

SERVES: 4-6

### SATAYS:

1¹/₂ lb (750 g) broiling (grilling) steak
1 medium onion, roughly chopped
1 teaspoon chopped garlic
1 teaspoon chopped fresh ginger
1¹/₂ teaspoons salt
¹/₂ teaspoon ground black pepper
1 stem fresh lemon grass, finely sliced or rind
of half a lemon, chopped
¹/₂ teaspoon ground fennel
4 candlenuts or 3 Brazil kernels, chopped
4 dried red chilies
¹/₂ teaspoon dried shrimp paste

### GRAVY:

1 medium onion, roughly chopped
1 teaspoon chopped garlic
1 teaspoon chopped fresh ginger
1 stem fresh lemon grass, chopped or rind
of half a lemon, chopped
2 teaspoons ground coriander
1 teaspoon ground cumin
¹/₂ teaspoon ground cinnamon
¹/₂ teaspoon ground cloves
¹/₂ teaspoon ground cardamom
4 candlenuts or 3 Brazil kernels, chopped
1 teaspoon dried shrimp paste
4 dried red chilies
1 teaspoon salt
¹/₂ teaspoon ground black pepper
3 tablespoons peanut oil
1 cup (8 fl oz, 250 ml) coconut cream

*Satays:* Cube steak and set aside in a bowl. Put
rest of ingredients in container of electric blender
and blend to a smooth paste, adding a little water
to facilitate blending. Marinate meat in this mixture for at least 30 minutes. Thread pieces of
meat on small bamboo skewers and broil (grill)

until well done, turning skewers so meat cooks
on all sides. Place on a dish, pour the gravy over
satays and serve with rice and accompaniments
such as sliced cucumber and onion, or Malay
pickles (see page 97).

*Gravy:* Put all ingredients, excepting coconut
cream and peanut oil, in container of electric
blender and blend to a smooth paste, adding a little water to facilitate blending.

Heat oil in a saucepan, stir in blended mixture
and cook until it smells aromatic. Add the
coconut cream and cook, stirring occasionally,
until it thickens and the oil comes to the surface.
Pour this gravy over the satays.

*Beef Smoore (page 29).*

*Fried Pork Curry (page 41).*

NORTH INDIA

# GROUND MEAT & POTATO CURRY

~

*GOOD AS A FILLING FOR CURRY PUFFS TOO! CHARMAINE.*

SERVES: 4–6

3 tablespoons oil or ghee
2 medium onions, finely chopped
1 teaspoon finely chopped garlic
1 teaspoon finely grated fresh ginger
$1/2$ teaspoon ground turmeric
2 teaspoons ground coriander
1 teaspoon ground cumin
$1/2$ teaspoon chili powder, optional
2 teaspoons salt
2 tablespoons lemon juice or vinegar
1 lb (500 g) ground lamb or beef
1 lb (500 g) potatoes, peeled and quartered
1 cup (8 fl oz, 250 ml) hot water
1 teaspoon garam masala (see page 12)

GARNISH:
2 tablespoons chopped fresh mint or cilantro
(fresh coriander leaves)

Heat oil in a heavy saucepan and fry the onions, garlic, and ginger until soft and golden. Add turmeric, coriander, cumin, and chili powder and fry, stirring, for 1 minute. Add the salt and lemon juice and when it starts to sizzle fry the meat, stirring constantly, until all the meat is browned and any lumps broken up.

Add the potatoes and hot water, bring to simmering point, cover and cook on low heat until potatoes are done and meat tender, about 30 minutes. Stir occasionally towards end of this time to ensure curry does not catch to base of pan. Sprinkle the garam masala over, stir gently, then garnish with the chopped herbs. Serve with rice or Indian breads.

MALAYSIA

# BEEF & TOASTED COCONUT CURRY

~

*THE TOASTED COCONUT MAKES FOR QUITE AN UNUSUAL CURRY. AT THE FOOD STALL IN KUALA LUMPUR THEY STEPPED UP THE CHILIES, GARLIC AND BLACHAN. REUBEN*

SERVES: 4–6

2 lb (1kg) lean stewing steak, thinly sliced
3 tablespoons peanut oil
3 tablespoons unsweetened desiccated coconut
1 stem lemon grass, chopped or rind of half lemon
4 dried red chilies
1 teaspoon chopped garlic
1 teaspoon chopped fresh ginger
1 medium onion, roughly chopped
1 teaspoon dried shrimp paste
4 tablespoons tamarind liquid (see Glossary)
2 teaspoons salt

Roast coconut in a dry pan till golden brown. Remove to a plate and when cool put into blender together with rest of ingredients and blend to a smooth paste adding a little hot water to facilitate blending.

Heat oil in a saucepan then add blended spices and cook, stirring till oil comes to the surface and spices smell aromatic. Add meat and stir till browned, then cover and simmer till meat is tender, stirring occasionally. Add more water if necessary.

Serve with rice and accompaniments.

*INDONESIA*

# SUMATRAN BEEF CURRY

∼

SERVES: 4–6

2 lb (1kg) lean stewing steak
1 large onion, roughly chopped
2 teaspoons chopped garlic
2 teaspoons ground coriander
2 teaspoons ground cumin
2 teaspoons dried shrimp paste
6 candlenuts or 4 Brazil nuts, chopped
8 dried red chilies
1 teaspoon laos powder
1 teaspoon ground turmeric
2 teaspoons salt
$^1/_2$ teaspoon ground black pepper
3 tablespoons peanut oil
1 cup (8 fl oz, 250 ml) coconut cream
4 tablespoons tamarind liquid (see Glossary)

Cube the steak and set aside in a bowl. Place onion, garlic, coriander, cumin, shrimp paste, nuts, chilies, laos powder, turmeric, salt, and pepper in container of electric blender and blend to a smooth paste, adding a little water to facilitate blending. Marinate meat in this mixture for 30 minutes.

Heat oil in a saucepan, stir in meat and marinade and cook till meat is browned. Cover and simmer on very low heat till meat is tender, stirring occasionally. Juices from the meat should provide sufficient liquid, but if necessary add a little water.

Add coconut cream and continue stirring till oil comes to the surface. Stir in tamarind liquid, cook a few more minutes uncovered and serve with rice and accompaniments.

*BURMA*

# BEEF & POTATO CURRY

∼

*BUDGET-STRETCHING, BURMESE STYLE. SOMETIMES PUMPKIN IS USED INSTEAD OF POTATO. CHARMAINE.*

SERVES: 4–6

$1^1/_2$ lb (750 g) beef
$3/4$ lb (375 g) potatoes
2 large onions
5 large cloves garlic
2 teaspoons chopped fresh ginger
1 teaspoon chili powder
8 tablespoons light sesame oil or corn oil
$^1/_2$ teaspoon ground cumin
$^1/_2$ teaspoon ground coriander
$1^1/_2$ teaspoons salt or to taste
2 cups (16 fl oz, 500 ml) water

Cut beef into large cubes. Peel and cut potatoes into quarters. Cook basic ingredients as described on page 18. When cooked and sizzling, add cumin and coriander, then add meat and fry, stirring for a few minutes. Add salt, about 2 cups (16 fl oz, 500 ml) water, potatoes and simmer slowly until meat is tender and potatoes are cooked.

*Note:* Some cooks prefer to rub the cumin, coriander, and salt into the beef before cooking. Care must be taken to fry on low heat so spices will not burn.

MALAYSIA

# HOT BEEF CURRY

∽

*WE ENJOYED THIS PARTICULAR DISH IN PENANG, AND THIS IS EXACTLY AS WE HAD IT. CHARMAINE AND REUBEN.*

SERVES: 4

1 lb (500 g) stewing steak
5 red or green chilies
1 large onion, roughly chopped
1 teaspoon chopped garlic
1 teaspoon chopped fresh ginger
$^1/4$ cup (1 oz, 300 g) roasted peanuts
$^1/2$ teaspoon ground nutmeg
$^1/2$ teaspoon ground black pepper
1 teaspoon salt
1 tablespoon lemon juice
1 cup (8 fl oz, 250 ml) warm water
2 tablespoons peanut oil
1 tablespoon light soy sauce
3 daun salam or curry leaves

Cut meat into 2 in (5 cm) squares. Into an electric blender put chilies, onion, garlic, ginger, peanuts, nutmeg, black pepper, salt, and lemon juice. Blend to a paste, adding a little warm water to facilitate blending.

Heat oil in a saucepan, add contents of blender and cook for 5 minutes, stirring occasionally. Add meat and cook for a further 5 minutes. Add soy sauce, daun salam, and rest of warm water, stir well, cover and simmer until meat is tender and oil comes to the top. Stir occasionally to prevent meat catching to base of saucepan. Adjust seasoning and serve with hot rice and a sambal.

INDIA

# SKEWERED MUTTON CURRY

∽

*CHARMAINE VERY SWEETLY ASKED ME TO TEST THIS RECIPE. I WONDERED WHY. JUST WATCH OUT FOR SKEWERED FINGERS! REUBEN.*

SERVES: 4–6

2 lb (1 kg) lamb or hogget
thin slices of fresh young ginger root
3 tablespoons ghee or oil
1 large onion, finely chopped
$1^1/2$ teaspoons finely chopped garlic
1 tablespoon ground coriander
2 teaspoons ground cumin
$^1/2$ teaspoon ground fennel
$^1/2$ teaspoon ground turmeric
$^1/2$ teaspoon ground black pepper
2 teaspoons salt
1 ripe tomato, diced
2 green chilies, sliced
$^1/2$ teaspoon ground cinnamon
$^1/2$ teaspoon ground cardamom
$^1/4$ teaspoon ground cloves

Cut meat into small cubes and thread on thin bamboo skewers which have been cut in 4 in (10 cm) lengths, alternating each piece of meat with a thin slice of ginger. Cut the ginger from a slender root so the slices will not be too big, or cut large slices in pieces.

Heat ghee or oil and fry onion over medium low heat until soft, stirring occasionally. Add garlic, stir and fry until onion is golden brown. Add coriander, cumin, fennel, turmeric, and pepper and fry for 1 minute, then add salt and tomato and stir for 3 minutes longer. Add chilies and skewered meat and fry until meat is lightly brown. Turn heat low, cover and cook until meat is tender. Liquid from the meat will eventually be re-absorbed, leaving the gravy very thick. Stir occasionally to prevent spices catching to the base of the pan.

Ten minutes before cooked sprinkle cinnamon, cardamom, and cloves over the curry. Stir well and leave on very low heat. Serve hot with rice.

*MALAYSIA*

# SPICY MUTTON CURRY

∾

SERVES: 6

1$^1$/$_2$ lb (750 g) hogget or lamb
4 tablespoons unsweetened desiccated coconut
1/4 cup (2 fl oz, 60 ml) tamarind liquid
(see Glossary)
2 large onions, roughly chopped
2 teaspoons chopped garlic
1 tablespoon roughly chopped fresh ginger
2 teaspoons ground coriander
1 teaspoon each ground cumin and turmeric
$^1$/$_2$ teaspoon each ground cinnamon, fennel,
nutmeg and black pepper
$^1$/$_4$ teaspoon each ground cloves and
cardamom
4 candlenuts
4-8 dried red chilies, or to taste
2 tablespoons peanut oil
2 ripe tomatoes, chopped
1$^1$/$_2$ cups (12 fl oz, 375 ml) coconut cream
1$^1$/$_2$ teaspoons salt
1 stem fresh lemon grass, finely sliced,
or 1 teaspoon finely chopped lemon rind

Cut meat into small cubes. Brown the coconut in a dry frying pan, stirring over medium low heat for 4 or 5 minutes or until it is golden-brown in color. Set aside. Pour $^1$/$_4$ cup (2 fl oz, 60 ml) hot water over a walnut-size piece of dried tamarind pulp and leave for 5 minutes. Squeeze the tamarind in the water to dissolve. Strain through a fine sieve.

In the container of an electric blender put the tamarind liquid and onions and blend to a smooth, thick liquid. Add the garlic and ginger and blend again. Add spices, candlenuts, dried chilies, and last of all, the toasted coconut. Blend until smooth and well combined.

Heat the oil in a large saucepan and fry the blended mixture for about 5 minutes, stirring frequently at the beginning and constantly at the end. Add meat and fry for 3 minutes, stirring so each piece is coated with spices. Add tomato and fry for 3 minutes. Add coconut cream, salt, and lemon grass and bring to a boil. Reduce heat to very low and simmer, uncovered, until meat is tender, stirring now and then. This may take 1$^1$/$_2$ to 2 hours.

*INDIA*

# LAMB KORMA
∾

*ONE OF THE CLASSIC DISHES OF INDIA AND WELL WORTH TRYING.*
*CHARMAINE.*

SERVES: 6

2 lb (1kg) boned leg of lamb
2 medium onions
1 tablespoon chopped fresh ginger
2 teaspoons chopped garlic
$^{1}/_{4}$ cup (1 oz, 30 g) raw cashews or
blanched almonds
2-6 dried chilies, seeded
2 teaspoons ground coriander
1 teaspoon ground cumin
$^{1}/_{4}$ teaspoon ground cinnamon
$^{1}/_{4}$ teaspoon ground cardamom
$^{1}/_{4}$ teaspoon ground cloves
$^{1}/_{2}$ teaspoon saffron strands or $^{1}/_{4}$ teaspoon
powdered saffron
2 tablespoons boiling water
1 tablespoon ghee
2 tablespoons oil
2 teaspoons salt
$^{1}/_{2}$ cup (4 fl oz, 125 ml) natural yogurt
2 tablespoons chopped cilantro
(fresh coriander leaves)

Cut lamb into large cubes, trimming off any excess fat. Peel onions, slice one finely and set aside. Chop other onion roughly and put into an electric blender with ginger, garlic, cashews, and chilies. Add $^{1}/_{2}$ cup (4 fl oz, 125 ml) water to blender, cover and blend on high speed for a minute or until all ingredients are ground smoothly. Add all the ground spices and blend for a few seconds longer.

Put the saffron strands into a small bowl, pour the boiling water over and allow to soak while starting to cook the masala (ground spice mixture).

Heat ghee and oil in a large saucepan and when hot put in the finely sliced onion and fry, stirring frequently with a wooden spoon, until soft and golden. Add the blended mixture and continue to fry, stirring constantly until the masala is well cooked and the oil starts to separate from the mixture. Wash out blender with an extra $^{1}/_{4}$ cup (2 fl oz, 60 ml) water, add to pan together with salt and continue to stir and fry until the liquid dries up once more.

Add the meat and stir over medium heat until each piece is coated with the spice. Stir the saffron, crushing the strands against side of the bowl, then add to the pan. Stir to mix well. Add yogurt and stir again until evenly mixed. Reduce heat to low, cover and cook at a gentle simmer for 1 hour or until meat is tender and gravy thick. Stir occasionally, taking care that the spice mixture does not catch to base of pan. When lamb is tender, sprinkle with cilantro, replace lid and cook for 5 minutes longer. Serve hot with rice.

*INDIA*

# MADRAS MUTTON CURRY

∾

*I SAID MORE CHILIES. NO, SHE SAID AND WON THE TOSS. I STILL SAY MORE CHILIES. REUBEN.*

SERVES: 6–8

3 lb (1.5 kg) lamb forequarter chops or other meat, cubed

3 tablespoons oil

10 curry leaves

3 medium onions, finely chopped

3 teaspoons chopped garlic

1 tablespoon finely chopped fresh ginger

1 teaspoon ground turmeric

3-4 teaspoons chili powder, or to taste

3 teaspoons ground coriander

1 teaspoon ground cumin

$2^1/_2$ teaspoons salt

2 tablespoons vinegar

2 or 3 fresh green chilies, split halfway from tip

2 tablespoons unsweetened desiccated coconut

$1^1/_2$ cups (12 fl oz, 375 ml) coconut cream

Cut chops in large pieces, keeping the bone in. Heat oil in a large heavy saucepan and fry the curry leaves until brown. Add onions, garlic, and ginger and fry until soft and golden. Add turmeric and fry for a few seconds, then put in chili powder, coriander, and cumin and fry for 1 minute.

Add salt and vinegar and stir until liquid evaporates, then put in the meat and stir until it is coated with the spices. Add green chilies, lower heat, cover and cook until the meat is tender. Juices come from the meat and there should be no need to add water.

Meanwhile, roast the coconut in a dry pan until golden brown. Grind finely in electric blender and if necessary add $^1/_2$ cup (4 fl oz, 125 ml) of the coconut cream to facilitate blending. Blend on high speed for 30 seconds. Add to the curry together with the rest of the coconut cream and simmer uncovered until gravy is thick. Serve with rice and accompaniments.

*IINDONESIA*

# DRY MEAT CURRY

∾

*THIS COMBINATION OF SPICES RESULTS IN TWO TYPES OF CURRY — ONE IS KALIO, WHICH HAS A VERY THICK GRAVY. THE OTHER IS RENDANG, WHEN COOKING IS CONTINUED UNTIL THE CONSISTENCY IS ALMOST DRY AND THE OIL SEPARATES FROM THE GRAVY. FOR KALIO, STOP COOKING AFTER ADDING THE THICK COCONUT CREAM AND BRINGING TO SIMMERING POINT. CHARMAINE.*

SERVES: 8

3 lb (1.5 kg ) beef or mutton

2 medium onions

2 cloves garlic

1 tablespoon chopped fresh ginger

3 tablespoons peanut oil

1 small stick cinnamon

4 or 5 whole cloves

3 teaspoons ground coriander

1 teaspoon ground cumin

1 teaspoon ground black pepper

I teaspoon chili powder, or to taste

$^1/_2$ teaspoon ground fennel

$^1/_2$ teaspoon ground kencur (aromatic ginger)

3 tablespoons unsweetened desiccated coconut, toasted

4 cups (32 fl oz, 1 L) thin coconut cream

2 teaspoons salt

$^1/_4$ cup (2 fl oz, 60 ml) tamarind liquid (see Glossary)

1 cup (8 fl oz, 250 ml) thick coconut cream

Cut meat into large cubes. Finely slice one onion and set aside. Roughly chop the other onion and put into a blender with garlic and ginger. Blend to a smooth purée, adding 2 tablespoons of the thin coconut cream. Put meat into a bowl, mix with ground ingredients, set aside.

In a large saucepan heat the oil and fry sliced onion and whole spices, stirring occasionally, until onion is soft and starts to turn golden. Add meat and fry until meat is browned. Add ground spices, coconut, thin coconut cream and salt. Stir while bringing to a boil and continue stirring for about 10 minutes. Simmer uncovered until meat is almost tender. Add tamarind liquid, stir well and simmer until liquid is almost dry. Add thick coconut cream, stirring constantly, and allow to simmer again until oil separates from gravy and curry is very dry.

*SRI LANKA*

# FRIED PORK CURRY

∾

*ONE OF THE MOST POPULAR DISHES IN SRI LANKA, ESPECIALLY ON FESTIVE OCCASIONS. CHARMAINE.*

SERVES: 6–8

2 lb (1 kg) pork belly or forequarter
3 tablespoons oil
10 curry leaves
$1/4$ teaspoon fenugreek seeds, optional
2 medium onions, finely chopped
2 teaspoons finely chopped garlic
$1^1/2$ teaspoons finely grated fresh ginger
3 tablespoons Ceylon curry powder (see page 12)
1-2 teaspoons chili powder
2 teaspoons salt
1 tablespoon vinegar
1 tablespoon tamarind pulp dissolved in $1^1/2$ cups
(12 fl oz, 375 ml) hot water
2 in (5 cm) cinnamon stick
4 cardamom pods
1 cup (8 fl oz, 250 ml) thick coconut cream

Cut pork into large cubes. Heat oil in a large saucepan and fry curry leaves and fenugreek, if used, until they start to brown. Add onion and garlic and fry over a low heat until soft and golden. Add ginger, curry powder, chili powder, salt, vinegar, and pork. Fry on high heat, stirring thoroughly until meat is well coated with the spice mixture. Squeeze tamarind pulp in hot water, strain and discard seeds. Add tamarind liquid, cinnamon, and cardamom, cover and cook on low heat until pork is tender, about 1 hour. Add coconut cream and cook 10 minutes or more, uncovered.

Pour gravy into another saucepan, return pork to heat and allow to fry in its own fat. (If pork is not fat enough, add 1 tablespoon of ghee or oil to pan.) When pork is nicely brown, return gravy to pan and cook, uncovered, until gravy is thick. Serve hot with boiled rice.

See picture opposite page 35.

*MALAYSIA*

# HOT PORK CURRY

∾

*I LIKE THIS! I SHOULD BE FORGIVEN! REUBEN.*

1 lb (500 g) forequarter of pork, boned
1 medium onion, roughly chopped
4 dried red chilies
3 fresh red chilies
4 candlenuts or 3 Brazil nuts, chopped
1 teaspoon dried shrimp paste
1 stem fresh lemon grass, sliced, or rind of $1/2$ lemon
1 teaspoon turmeric
4 tablespoons peanut oil
1 cup (8 fl oz, 250 ml) pork or chicken stock
1 teaspoon sugar
1 tablespoon vinegar
1 teaspoon salt
1 large onion, finely sliced
2 teaspoons chopped garlic
1 tablespoon chopped fresh ginger

Cut pork into cubes and set aside. Place chopped onion, dried and fresh chilies, nuts, shrimp paste, lemon grass, and turmeric in blender and blend to a paste, adding a little stock to facilitate blending. Heat 2 tablespoons oil in a saucepan and fry spice mixture for 3 to 4 minutes. Add meat and stir-fry till browned all over. Stir in stock, sugar, vinegar, and salt and simmer covered until pork is cooked and liquid almost absorbed.

In another saucepan, heat remaining oil and fry the sliced onion, garlic, and ginger till soft and golden brown. Add this to saucepan containing pork, bring to a boil and serve with rice.

*SOUTH INDIA*

# PORK VINDALOO

∾

*VINDALOO DENOTES A HOT, SOUR PREPARATION WHICH PRESERVES MEAT WITHOUT REFRIGERATION FOR A FEW DAYS.*

2 lb (1 kg) pork
6-8 large dried red chilies
1 cup (8 fl oz, 250 ml) vinegar, preferably coconut vinegar
2 teaspoons chopped fresh ginger
4 teaspoons chopped garlic
2 teaspoons ground cumin
$1/2$ teaspoon ground black pepper
$1/2$ teaspoon ground cinnamon
$1/2$ teaspoon ground cardamom
$1/4$ teaspoon ground cloves
$1/4$ teaspoon ground nutmeg
2 teaspoons salt
2-3 tablespoons ghee or oil
2 medium onions, finely chopped
1 tablespoon brown sugar

Cut pork into cubes. Soak chilies in vinegar for 10 minutes. If available use coconut vinegar for authentic taste, but any kind of vinegar may be substituted, diluting it if it is very strong. Put chilies and vinegar, ginger, garlic, all the ground spices, and salt into electric blender and blend until chilies are finely ground. Pour this mixture over the pork in an earthenware bowl, cover and marinate for 2 hours.

Heat enough ghee or oil to cover base of an enamel or stainless steel saucepan. (This dish is cooked in earthenware pots in India and if one is available it would be an advantage.) Fry the onions on low heat until soft and golden, stirring frequently. Drain pork from the marinade and fry on medium high heat, stirring, until lightly brown. Pour in marinade, cover pan and simmer on low heat until pork is tender, about $1^1/2$ hours. Stir in sugar. Serve with plain white rice.

*BURMA*

# PORK CURRY, DRY

∾

*I SNEAKED THIS ONE IN, ANOTHER OF MY FAVORITES. REUBEN.*

SERVES: 4

1 lb (500 g) pork
1 large onion
3 cloves garlic
1 teaspoon finely grated fresh ginger
$1/2$ teaspoon chili powder
$1/2$ teaspoon ground turmeric
3 tablespoons light sesame oil or corn oil
1 stem lemon grass or 2 strips lemon rind
2 tablespoons tamarind liquid (see Glossary)
1 teaspoon salt
1 tablespoon fish sauce (see Glossary)

Cut pork into 2 in (5 cm) pieces. Excess fat should be removed or the curry will be too rich, but some fat left on the meat is quite acceptable.

Purée and cook onion, garlic, ginger, chili, and turmeric as described on page 18. When well cooked, add pork and simmer gently in its own juice until tender. In blender purée chopped lemon grass or rind, tamarind juice, salt, and fish sauce. Add to pan and stir well. Cook until all water has evaporated and the oil separates from the gravy.

You can vary the taste of the curry by adding extra chili powder for a hot curry, or stirring in a piece of hot Indian mango pickle, chopped cilantro (fresh coriander leaves) or chopped scallions (spring onions).

# PORK PADRÉ CURRY

~

# PORK CURRY

~

SERVES: 8

*I NOTICE THAT IN SRI LANKAN COOKERY, WHENEVER A CURRY
HAS THAT "SECRET" INGREDIENT, ARRACK, IT BECOMES A PADRÉ
CURRY. PERHAPS THIS WAS THE PADRÉ'S ONLY OPPORTUNITY
TO IMBIBE! WHISKY MAY BE USED INSTEAD OF ARRACK,
A SPIRIT DISTILLED FROM COCONUT PALMS. CHARMAINE.*

SERVES: 6–8

3 lb (1.5 kg) pork forequarter, boned
1 tablespoon ground coriander
2 teaspoons ground cumin
1 teaspoon fennel seeds
2 large onions, sliced
2 teaspoons chopped fresh ginger
2 teaspoons chopped garlic
rind of half a lemon
2 teaspoons chili powder
12 curry leaves
1 stick of cinnamon
$^1/_4$ cup (2 fl oz, 60 ml) whisky or arrack
1 tablespoon sugar
$^1/_2$ teaspoon pepper
3 teaspoons salt
2 cups (16 fl oz, 500 ml) thick coconut cream
$^1/_4$ cup (2 fl oz, 60 ml) tamarind liquid or vinegar
(see Glossary)

Cube pork and set aside. Roast the coriander, cumin, and fennel (or use a dark roasted Ceylon curry powder). Put spices into blender together with onions, ginger, garlic, lemon rind, chili powder, and curry leaves. Add 1 cup (8 fl oz, 250 ml) of water and blend to a smooth paste. Put blended mixture and pork into a saucepan and add one cup (8 fl oz, 250 ml) of the coconut cream, the cinnamon, pepper, salt, and tamarind. Bring to a boil, cover and simmer for 50 minutes.

Add sugar and whisky and simmer until pork is tender. If more liquid is needed, add a little hot water. Towards end of cooking time add remaining coconut cream and simmer, uncovered, until thick. Serve with rice and accompaniments.

2 lb (1 kg) pork belly
8–10 large dried chilies
$1^1/_2$ cups (12 fl oz, 375 ml) hot water
1 tablespoon tamarind pulp
$^1/_2$ teaspoon ground turmeric
1 medium onion, roughly chopped
5 cloves garlic
$1^1/_2$ teaspoons chopped fresh ginger
2 in (5 cm) cinnamon stick
2 teaspoons salt
1 stem lemon grass or 2 strips lemon rind
10 curry leaves
$^1/_4$ teaspoon fenugreek seeds
1 strip daun pandan leaf (rampé), optional
$^1/_2$ cup (4 fl oz, 125 ml) thick coconut cream
1 tablespoon oil or melted ghee
1 small onion, finely sliced
2 tablespoons lemon juice

Cut the pork into 2 in (5 cm) pieces and put into a saucepan. Remove stalks and seeds from dried chilies and soak them in half the hot water for 10 minutes. Soak and dissolve tamarind pulp in remaining hot water, strain out seeds and fibers. Put chilies and soaking water into blender with the turmeric, roughly chopped onion, garlic, and ginger and blend until smooth. Pour over pork in pan, add cinnamon and strained tamarind water. Add salt, half each of the lemon grass, curry leaves, fenugreek seeds, and pandan leaf. Bring to a boil, then turn heat low, cover and simmer until pork is tender. Add coconut cream and simmer, uncovered, for 10 minutes longer.

In another pan heat the oil or ghee and fry the sliced onion and the remaining lemon grass, curry leaves, fenugreek seeds, and pandan. When onion is golden brown, transfer to the cooked pork mixture and add the lemon juice, stir and simmer on very low heat for about 5 minutes. Serve with rice and accompaniments.

# DRY-FRIED KIDNEY CURRY

∾

SERVES: 6

1¹/₂ lb (750 g) ox kidney
1 teaspoon finely grated fresh ginger
1 teaspoon finely chopped garlic
1 teaspoon salt
3 tablespoons peanut oil
2 onions, finely chopped or sliced
1 teaspoon ground turmeric
2 teaspoons ground coriander
1 teaspoon ground cumin
¹/₂ teaspoon ground fennel
¹/₂ teaspoon ground black pepper
1 teaspoon chili powder or 2 fresh red chilies,
seeded and chopped
3 candlenuts, finely grated
2 cups (16 fl oz, 500 ml) coconut cream
1 small stick cinnamon
2 tablespoons tamarind liquid
2 teaspoons sugar

Wash kidneys, remove and discard core. Cut kidneys into small dice. Rub with ginger and garlic crushed with salt and set aside.

Heat oil and fry onions until they are soft and start to turn golden, stirring frequently. Add turmeric, coriander, cumin, fennel and pepper and stir-fry for 1 minute. Add chilies, candlenuts and kidneys, continue to fry, stirring constantly, until kidneys are browned. Add coconut cream and cinnamon and simmer gently, uncovered, until gravy is thick and reduced. This will take almost 2 hours of gentle simmering. Stir occasionally during simmering period. As mixture thickens it will be necessary to stir more frequently. Add tamarind liquid and sugar, stir and cook for a few minutes longer. Serve hot.

# LIVER CURRY

∾

SERVES: 4–6

2 lb (1 kg) calves' liver, diced
2 tablespoons unsweetened desiccated coconut
2 teaspoons chopped garlic
4 candlenuts or 3 Brazil kernels, chopped
4 fresh red chilies
2 teaspoons ground coriander
1 teaspoon ground cumin
1 teaspoon ground fennel
1 stem lemon grass chopped or 2 strips lemon rind
2 teaspoons dried shrimp paste
1¹/₂ teaspoons salt
4 tablespoons peanut oil
1 large onion, thinly sliced
¹/₂ cup (4 fl oz, 125 ml) coconut cream

Roast desiccated coconut in a dry pan until golden brown. Remove to a plate and when cool put into blender with the garlic, nuts, chilies, coriander, cumin, fennel, lemon grass, shrimp paste, and salt. Blend to a smooth paste adding a little hot water to facilitate blending.

Heat oil in a saucepan and fry onion till soft and golden. Add blended spices and fry till they smell aromatic and oil comes to the surface. Add diced liver and coconut cream and simmer till cooked, stirring contents occasionally. Serve with rice and accompaniments.

SRI LANKA

# LIVER CURRY

∾

*EVEN PEOPLE WHO DON'T LIKE EATING LIVER FIND IT MOST PALATABLE WHEN PREPARED THIS WAY. CHARMAINE.*

SERVES: 4

1 lb (500 g) calves' liver, sliced
10 black peppercorns
1 teaspoon salt
1 tablespoon ghee or oil
1 medium onion, finely chopped
1 1/2 teaspoons finely chopped garlic
1 teaspoon finely chopped fresh ginger
1 stem lemon grass or 2 strips lemon rind
1/4 teaspoon ground cloves
1/2 teaspoon ground black pepper
1/2 teaspoon ground cinnamon
8 curry leaves
3 tablespoons vinegar
2 cups (16 fl oz, 500 ml) coconut cream
2 tablespoons chopped fresh dill or 1/2 teaspoon dried dill weed

Wash liver, put into small saucepan with water to cover, add peppercorns and salt and cook until liver is firm, about 15 minutes. Cool.

Cut liver into very small dice. Heat ghee or oil and fry onion, garlic, and ginger until soft. Add all ingredients, including liver, and cook uncovered over a low heat until gravy is thick.

SRI LANKA

# TRIPE CURRY

∾

*A GREAT MANY INGREDIENTS. TRUE. BUT THE END PRODUCT IS WORTH THE EFFORT. REUBEN.*

SERVES: 6

2 lb (1 kg) tripe
8 large dried chilies
1/2 cup (4 fl oz, 125 ml) hot water
2 teaspoons ground cumin
1/2 teaspoon ground turmeric
1/2 teaspoon fenugreek seeds
1/2 teaspoon aromatic ginger (kencur)
8 curry leaves
1 stem lemon grass or 2 strips lemon rind
1 strip dried daun pandan (rampé)
8 whole cardamom pods
4 whole cloves
1 small stick cinnamon
2 medium onions, finely chopped
2 teaspoons finely chopped garlic
1 1/2 teaspoons finely grated fresh ginger
2 cups (16 fl oz, 500 ml) thin coconut cream
1 1/2 teaspoons salt
1 cup (8 fl oz, 250 ml) thick coconut cream
2 tablespoons lemon juice

Wash tripe well and cut into 2 in (5 cm) squares. After removing stalks and seeds, soak chilies in the hot water for 10 minutes, then blend in electric blender until pulverized. Alternatively, use 2 teaspoons chili powder.

Put tripe and all other ingredients except thick coconut cream and lemon juice, into a large saucepan and bring to a boil. Cover and simmer for 1 1/2 hours or until tripe is tender and gravy smooth and thickened. Add thick coconut cream and simmer, uncovered, stirring for 10 minutes. Remove from heat add lemon juice and serve with rice.

# FISH & SEAFOOD

AN ABUNDANCE OF seafood in coastal areas keeps many millions of Asian people supplied with protein. They eat the fish fresh and they also salt it and dry it in the sun or pickle it in brine. In very poor areas, the diet is literally rice and fish. In dried and salted form fish is part of every meal, sometimes simply fried in a little coconut oil and nibbled at to make the plain rice more interesting.

Even in more affluent circles, salt fish is prepared as an accompaniment. This is cooked with fried onions and dried chilies in a fiery but irresistible sambal.

Fresh fish, shrimps, crabs, and other sea creatures are more to western taste, however, and they may be curried in as many ways as there are imaginative cooks. Mild coconut cream curries with gentle spices, or hot curries with lots of chili, or piquant curries with tamarind or vinegar — all have their advocates.

Delicate fish are best cooked in mild curries, but for strong tasting fish, try the hot and sour curries.

While small fish such as sprats, anchovies and sardines are cooked whole, larger fish are cut into serving pieces. Filets are no problem to divide into portions, but when it comes to fish steaks there is a special way they are cut for curry: small or medium steaks may simply be halved crosswise, but larger fish steaks are cut into four, six or eight.

SRI LANKA

# FISH CURRY WITH TOMATO

∽

*THERE ARE MANY TYPES OF FISH CURRY IN SRI LANKA — SOME MILD, SOME HOT, SOME VERY ACID, SOME MILDLY PIQUANT. THIS COMES IN THE FINAL CATEGORY. CHARMAINE.*

SERVES: 4–5

1 lb (500 g) fish steaks, kingfish, halibut, tuna, Spanish mackerel, mullet
1 teaspoon ground turmeric
1 teaspoon salt oil for frying
1 large onion, roughly chopped
3 cloves garlic
2 teaspoons finely chopped fresh ginger
1 medium size ripe tomato, chopped
2 tablespoons oil
1 tablespoon Ceylon curry powder (see page 12)
1 teaspoon chili powder
salt to taste
2 cups (16 fl oz, 500 ml) coconut cream

Wash and dry fish well and rub all over with turmeric and salt. Cut each steak into serving pieces. Heat oil in a frying pan and fry the fish until golden brown on both sides. Drain.

Put onion, garlic, ginger, and tomato in blender and blend to a smooth paste. Heat oil in a saucepan and fry the blended ingredients for a few minutes, until oil begins to separate from mixture. Add the curry and chili powders, and about a teaspoon of salt, then the coconut cream, and bring to a boil, stirring. Simmer for a few minutes, then add the fish and simmer for 10 minutes. Serve with rice and accompaniments.

INDIA

# FISH CURRY

∽

SERVES 4

1 lb (500 g) fish steaks or filets or small whole fish
2 tablespoons oil
6–8 curry leaves
1 medium onion, finely sliced
1 teaspoon finely chopped garlic
1 tablespoon finely grated fresh ginger
1 tablespoon ground coriander
2 teaspoons ground cumin
$1/2$ teaspoon ground turmeric
$1/2$–1 teaspoon chili powder
$1/2$ teaspoon ground fenugreek
2 cups (16 fl oz, 500 ml) coconut cream
$1^1/2$ teaspoons salt or to taste
lemon juice to taste

Wash fish well. If small fish are used, clean and scale them. If large steaks or filets are used, cut them into serving pieces. Heat oil and fry the curry leaves until slightly brown, then add onion, garlic, and ginger and fry until onion is soft and golden. Add all the ground spices and fry, stirring, until they smell aromatic. Add coconut cream and salt and bring to a boil, stirring.

Simmer uncovered for 10 minutes, then put in the fish, ladle the liquid over it and simmer until fish is cooked, approximately 10 to 15 minutes. Remove from heat and stir in lemon juice to taste.

## BURMA
# FISH BALL CURRY
∼

*THE FISH CURRY WE BOTH LOVE BEST, VERY TASTY AND WELL
WORTH THE EXTRA TROUBLE OF MAKING THE FISH BALLS. THIS
RECIPE WAS TAUGHT TO ME BY MY GRANDMOTHER, ALICE GRAY,
WHO WAS BORN AND LIVED MOST OF HER LIFE IN BURMA.
CHARMAINE.*

SERVES: 6

FISH BALLS:

2 lb (1 kg) halibut (jewfish) or cod filets
$2^1/_2$ teaspoons salt
$^1/_2$ teaspoon pepper
1 medium onion, finely chopped
$^1/_2$ teaspoon finely chopped garlic
$1^1/_2$ teaspoons finely grated fresh ginger
2 tablespoons lemon juice, strained
1 tablespoon finely chopped cilantro
(fresh coriander leaves) or dill
2 slices white bread, soaked in hot water and
squeezed dry
1 tablespoon fish sauce (see Glossary) or
1 teaspoon anchovy paste or sauce, optional

CURRY:

$^1/_4$ cup (2 fl oz, 60 ml) light sesame oil or corn oil
3 medium onions, finely chopped
3 teaspoons finely chopped garlic
1 tablespoon finely chopped fresh ginger
1 teaspoon ground turmeric
1-2 teaspoons chili powder, optional
1 teaspoon paprika, optional
2 tomatoes, peeled and chopped
$1^1/_2$ teaspoons salt
1 teaspoon dried shrimp paste
$1^1/_2$ cups (12 fl oz, 375 ml) hot water
2 tablespoons chopped cilantro (fresh coriander leaves)
2 tablespoons lemon juice

*Fish Balls:* With a sharp knife remove skin from
fish. Finely grind (mince) fish, taking care to
remove bones. (To do this without a grinder
[mincer], cut filets in thin slices lengthwise, then
chop finely across.) Put ground fish in a large
bowl, add remaining ingredients. Mix thoroughly
with the hands. Shape the mixture into walnut
size balls (this quantity should make 24 balls).

*Curry:* Heat oil in large saucepan and fry onion,
garlic, and ginger until soft and golden. Add
turmeric, remove from heat and add chili powder
and paprika (if used), tomato, and salt. (In Burmese cooking the amount of chili used would be
enough to turn the gravy red, but the paprika is
suggested here as a substitute for a portion of it,
with chili used to suit individual tastes.)

Wrap dried shrimp paste in aluminium foil and
cook under hot broiler (griller) for a few minutes
on each side. Unwrap, dissolve in hot water and
add to the gravy. Cook gravy until tomato is soft
and pulpy. If gravy seems too reduced, add a little hot water. There should be enough gravy to
almost cover the fish balls.

Gently put the fish balls in the gravy and simmer over a moderate heat until they are cooked,
about 20 minutes. Shake pan gently from time to
time. Do not stir until fish is cooked and firm or
the balls might break. Stir in the chopped cilantro
and lemon juice and cook 5 minutes longer. Serve
with white rice and balachaung (see page 95).

See picture opposite page 35.

## THAILAND
# GREEN CURRY OF FISH
∼

*THE PREDOMINANCE OF FRESH HERBS GIVES THIS CURRY A
GREENISH TINT AND A GOOD FLAVOR. CHARMAINE*

SERVES: 4

1 lb (500 g) fish steaks
$2^1/_2$ cups (20 fl oz) coconut cream
2 tablespoons green curry paste (see page 13)
2 sprigs citrus leaves
1 teaspoon salt
1 tablespoon fish sauce (see Glossary)
1 or 2 green chilies, seeded and chopped
2 tablespoons finely chopped fresh basil

Wash fish and trim any spines with kitchen scis-
sors. Bring coconut cream to a boil with the curry
paste, stirring constantly. Add fish, reduce heat and
simmer with citrus leaves, salt and fish sauce until
the fish is cooked through, about 15 minutes.

Add chilies and fresh basil and simmer a few
minutes longer, then serve with white rice.

See picture on half title page.

*INDONESIA*

# SQUID CURRY

~

SERVES 4

1 lb (500 g) fresh squid
1 medium onion, finely chopped
1 teaspoon finely chopped garlic
1 teaspoon finely grated fresh ginger
1 teaspoon salt
1 teaspoon chili powder
$^1/_2$ teaspoon dried shrimp paste
$1^3/_4$ cups (14 fl oz) coconut cream
4 candlenuts or Brazil nuts, grated
1 stem lemon grass, finely sliced or 1 teaspoon grated lemon rind
1 teaspoon sugar
4 tablespoons tamarind liquid (see Glossary) or lemon juice to taste

Clean squid, removing head and ink sac. Wash well inside and out and rub away spotted skin from body. Cut each squid in halves lengthwise, then into bitesize pieces. Put all other ingredients except sugar and tamarind or lemon into a saucepan and bring to simmering point, stirring. Allow to simmer, uncovered, until thickened. Stir occasionally. Add squid, simmer for 5 to 6 minutes. Add sugar and tamarind or lemon juice, taste and add more salt if necessary. Serve hot with rice and vegetables.

*INDIA*

# FISH CURRY WITH FENUGREEK LEAVES

~

SERVES: 4

1 lb (500 g) fish filets
1 large onion, finely sliced
2 tablespoons peanut oil
1 teaspoon finely chopped garlic
1 teaspoon finely chopped fresh ginger
2 teaspoons curry leaves
1 tablespoon dried fenugreek leaves
1 teaspoon ground turmeric
1 teaspoon chili powder
$^1/_2$ teaspoon ground cardamom
$^1/_2$ teaspoon ground cinnamon
pinch of ground cloves
rind of half a lemon
$^1/_4$ cup (2 fl oz, 60 ml) thick coconut cream
$1^1/_2$ (12 fl oz, 375 ml) cups warm water
salt to taste

Heat oil and fry sliced onion till golden brown. Lower heat, add garlic, ginger, curry leaves, fenugreek leaves, turmeric, chili powder, cardamom, cinnamon, cloves, and lemon rind. Stir for 2 minutes then add coconut cream with the warm water. Add salt, stir and simmer for 10 minutes. Add fish, ensuring it is coated with the sauce, and simmer until fish is cooked. Serve with rice or Indian bread.

*INDIA*

# FISH KORMA

∾

*A VERY RICH DISH, TYPICAL OF NORTH INDIA. REUBEN.*

SERVES: 4–6

1¹/₂ lb (750 g) fish filets
lemon juice
1 teaspoon salt
1 teaspoon ground black pepper
1 teaspoon ground turmeric oil for frying
1 large onion, finely sliced
1 medium onion, roughly chopped
1 teaspoon chopped garlic
1 tablespoon chopped fresh ginger
2 or 3 fresh red chilies, seeded
2 tablespoons blanched almonds
1 tablespoon white poppy seeds, optional
2 teaspoons ground cumin
2 teaspoons ground coriander
¹/₄ teaspoon ground cardamom
¹/₄ teaspoon ground cinnamon
small pinch ground cloves
¹/₄ teaspoon saffron strands
2 tablespoons boiling water
¹/₂ cup (4 fl oz, 125 ml) natural yogurt
salt to taste
2 tablespoons chopped cilantro
(fresh coriander leaves)

Wash and dry fish, cut into large serving pieces and rub with lemon juice, salt, pepper, and turmeric. Heat oil in a shallow frying pan and on high heat brown the fish quickly on both sides. Lift out onto a plate. In the same oil fry the sliced onion until golden brown, remove and set aside.

Put chopped onion, garlic, ginger, chilies, almonds, poppy seeds into blender and purée. If necessary add a little water. Add ground spices and blend once more, briefly.

Pour off all but about 2 tablespoons oil from pan and fry the blended mixture until color changes and it gives out a pleasing aroma. It should be stirred constantly while frying and care taken that it does not catch to the pan and burn. Add ¹/₄ cup (2 fl oz, 60 ml) water to blender and swirl out any remaining spice mixture. Add to pan.

Pound saffron strands in mortar and pestle, add boiling water and stir, add to mixture in pan. Add yogurt, stir and simmer gently for a few minutes, then add fish pieces, turning them carefully in the sauce. Add salt to taste. Cover and simmer for about 10 minutes, then sprinkle with fresh coriander and serve hot with rice.

*INDIA*

# FISH WHITE CURRY

∾

*FOR CHILDREN, LEAVE OUT THE GREEN CHILIES — THE COCONUT CREAM GRAVY GIVES FLAVOR TO PLAIN STEAMED RICE. CHARMAINE.*

1¹/₂ lb (750 g) fish filets or steaks
lemon juice
1 teaspoon ground turmeric
1¹/₂ teaspoons salt
2 tablespoons oil or ghee
2 small onions, finely sliced
2 teaspoons finely sliced garlic
3 slices fresh ginger, cut into slivers
8-10 curry leaves
3 fresh green chilies, seeded and cut in half lengthwise
2 cups (16 fl oz, 500 ml) thin coconut cream
1 cup (8 fl oz, 250 ml) thick coconut cream
lime or lemon juice to taste
salt to taste

Wash the fish and rub over with lemon juice, turmeric and salt.

Heat the oil in a saucepan and on low heat fry the onions, garlic, ginger, curry leaves, and chilies until onions are soft. Stir frequently and do not allow any of the ingredients to brown. Add the thin coconut cream and stir while it comes to simmering point. Add the fish and cook slowly, uncovered, for 10 minutes.

Add thick coconut cream, stir gently, heat through and remove from heat, then add lime or lemon juice and salt to taste. Serve with white rice and a coconut chutney.

*Balinese Style Fish (page 53).*

*Fish Ball Curry (page 48), Chicken Curry with Noodles (page 70), and Dry Balachaung,*
*a popular Burmese accompaniment (page 95).*

*INDONESIA*

# FISH IN COCONUT CREAM & SPICES

∾

SERVES: 6

1¹/₂ lb (750 g) firm dark fish steaks
(tuna, mackerel, kingfish)
salt to taste
juice of half a lemon
2 onions, finely chopped
1¹/₂ teaspoons finely chopped garlic
2 teaspoons finely grated fresh ginger
1 teaspoon ground turmeric
¹/₂ teaspoon dried shrimp paste
1 teaspoon sambal ulek (see Glossary)
or chili powder
1 stem lemon grass or 2 strips lemon rind
1 teaspoon salt
1¹/₂ cups (12 fl oz, 375 ml) thin coconut cream
2 tablespoons chopped fresh basil
¹/₄ cup (2 fl oz, 60 ml) tamarind liquid (see Glossary)
1 cup (8 fl oz, 250 ml) thick coconut cream

Wash fish, rub with a little salt and lemon juice and set aside. Combine onions, garlic, ginger, turmeric, shrimp paste, sambal ulek, lemon grass, and salt in a saucepan with thin coconut cream. Bring to simmering point and simmer uncovered until onions are soft and liquid thickened.

Add fish, basil, and tamarind liquid and simmer until fish is cooked. Stir in the thick coconut cream and heat through but do not boil, stirring so that coconut cream does not curdle. Serve with white rice, vegetables, and sambals.

*SRI LANKA*

# FISH CURRY WITH TAMARIND

∾

SERVES: 4

1 lb (500 g) firm fish steaks or filets
1 rounded tablespoon tamarind pulp
¹/₂ cup (4 fl oz, 125 ml) hot water
1¹/₂ tablespoons Ceylon curry powder (see page 12)
1 teaspoon salt
¹/₄ teaspoon ground turmeric
1 teaspoon chili powder
3 tablespoons oil
6 curry leaves
¹/₄ teaspoon fenugreek seeds
1 medium onion, finely chopped
1 teaspoon finely chopped garlic

Wash and dry fish and cut into serving pieces. Soak tamarind pulp in hot water, allow to cool, squeeze to dissolve pulp. Strain through fine nylon sieve and discard seeds and fibers. Combine tamarind liquid with curry powder, salt, turmeric, chili powder, and marinate fish for 20 minutes.

Heat oil and fry the curry leaves and fenugreek seeds until golden brown, then add onion and garlic and continue to fry on medium heat until onion is golden, stirring occasionally. Add fish and marinade. Cover and cook over low heat for 10 minutes. Uncover and cook for a further 10 minutes. Serve with white rice and vegetable curries.

*MALAYSIA*

# FISH CURRY
∾

SERVES: 4

1 lb (500 g) firm fish steaks

2 medium onions, roughly chopped

2 cloves garlic

2 teaspoons chopped fresh ginger

1 teaspoon sambal ulek (see Glossary) or chili powder

1 cup (8 fl oz, 250 ml) thin coconut cream (milk)

1 tablespoon ground coriander

1 teaspoon ground cumin

$^1/_2$ teaspoon ground fennel

$^1/_2$ teaspoon ground turmeric

1 stem fresh lemon grass or 2 strips thinly peeled lemon rind

6 curry leaves

2 tablespoons lemon juice

1 teaspoon salt

$^1/_2$ cup (4 fl oz, 125 ml) thick coconut cream

Cut fish steaks into serving pieces. Put onions, garlic, ginger, and sambal ulek into blender and blend to a smooth paste, adding a tablespoon of thin coconut cream if necessary. Scrape the blended mixture into a saucepan, wash out blender with the thin coconut cream and add to saucepan together with the ground spices, lemon rind, and curry leaves.

Bring to a boil, reduce heat and simmer for about 8 minutes, then add the fish, tamarind liquid, and salt and simmer for 5 minutes. Add thick coconut cream and stir gently until curry reaches simmering point once more. Serve with rice.

*INDONESIA*

# HOT FISH CURRY WITH SHRIMP PASTE
∾

SERVES: 4

1 lb (500 g) fish filets

2 tablespoons oil

1 large onion, sliced

1 teaspoon dried shrimp paste

1 teaspoon finely chopped garlic

2 tablespoons ground roasted peanuts or crunchy peanut butter

1 teaspoon ground cumin

4 green chilies, chopped or 2 teaspoons chili powder

1 teaspoon turmeric

1 teaspoon laos powder

$^1/_2$ cup (4 fl oz, 125 ml) hot water

$^1/_4$ cup (2 fl oz, 60 ml) thick coconut cream

salt to taste

Heat oil in a saucepan and brown sliced onion on medium heat. Add shrimp paste and garlic, lower heat and stir for a few minutes. Add ground peanuts, cumin, chili, turmeric, and laos powder and cook 1 minute longer.

Add water, then stir, cover and simmer till mixture smells cooked and the oil comes to the top. Add coconut cream and salt, stir and add fish. Cover and simmer about 10 minutes and serve with steamed rice.

## INDIA

# FISH CURRY
# WITH COCONUT

∽

*SOME OF THE FINEST DISHES WE EVER HAD WERE AT THE BEACH
RESORTS IN GOA, MADRAS, MAHABALIPURAM, AND BOMBAY.
REUBEN.*

*IN SOUTH INDIA THEY WOULD USE COCONUT OIL INSTEAD OF
GHEE; AND IN BENGAL MUSTARD OIL PROVIDES THE FLAVOR
TYPICAL OF THE COOKING OF THAT AREA. BUT FOR THOSE
WHO ARE NOT USED TO THESE DISTINCTIVE OILS, GHEE
(CLARIFIED BUTTER) OR A LIGHT, NEUTRAL OIL (NOT OLIVE
OIL) IS MORE ACCEPTABLE. CHARMAINE.*

SERVES: 6

1¹/₂ lb (750 g) fish steaks
lemon juice, salt and pepper
6 large dried red chilies
2 tablespoons unsweetened desiccated coconut
1 tablespoon coriander seeds
2 teaspoons cumin seeds
¹/₄ teaspoon fenugreek seeds
4 teaspoons finely chopped garlic
1 teaspoon finely chopped fresh ginger
1 tablespoon tamarind pulp or 1 teaspoon
instant tamarind
¹/₂ cup (4 fl oz, 125 ml) hot water
2 tablespoons ghee or oil
1 large onion, finely chopped
1¹/₂ cups (12 fl oz, 375 ml) coconut cream
1¹/₂ teaspoons salt

Wash fish, rub over with lemon juice, salt, and pepper and set aside. Soak the chilies in hot water for 10 minutes.

In a dry pan roast the coconut, stirring constantly until brown. Remove coconut to a plate and dry roast the coriander, cumin, and fenugreek seeds, shaking pan or stirring, until brown. Put the chilies, coconut, spices, garlic, and ginger into a blender and blend to a smooth paste, adding a little water if necessary. Soak tamarind pulp in hot water, squeeze to dissolve, strain. Or dissolve instant tamarind in hot water. Reserve tamarind liquid.

Heat ghee in a heavy saucepan and fry the chopped onion until soft. Add the ground mixture and fry on medium heat, stirring, until it darkens and smells cooked. Add the coconut cream, salt, tamarind liquid and bring slowly to simmering point, stirring to prevent curdling. Add the fish and simmer for 10 minutes or until fish is cooked. Do not cover. Serve hot with rice.

*Note:* Ground coriander, cumin, and fenugreek may be used instead of whole seeds, but roast them on a low heat, stirring constantly and taking care that they do not burn.

## INDONESIA

# BALINESE
# STYLE FISH

∽

SERVES: 6

2 lb (1 kg) fish steaks
2 tablespoons peanut oil
2 medium onions, finely chopped
1 teaspoon finely chopped garlic
1¹/₂ teaspoons finely grated fresh ginger
1¹/₂ teaspoons sambal ulek (see Glossary)
or fresh chili paste
1 teaspoon finely grated lemon rind
1 teaspoon laos powder
2 tablespoons lemon juice
2 tablespoons palm sugar (see Glossary)
or substitute
2 tablespoons dark soy sauce
¹/₂ teaspoon salt
peanut oil for frying

Wash fish, dry on absorbent paper towels and cut into serving portions. Heat about 2 tablespoons oil in a small saucepan and fry the onions until soft. Add garlic and ginger and stir over medium heat until golden brown. Add sambal ulek, lemon rind, laos powder, lemon juice, sugar, soy sauce, and salt and simmer for 2 or 3 minutes. Set aside.

Heat peanut oil for deep frying and fry the fish until golden brown on both sides. Drain, put on serving plate and spoon the sauce over. Serve with rice.

See picture opposite page 50.

SRI LANKA

# FRIED SQUID CURRY

∾

SERVES: 4–6

about 2 lb (1 kg) squid

2 medium onions, finely sliced

2 teaspoons finely chopped garlic

2 teaspoons finely grated fresh ginger

1 teaspoon ground turmeric

1 teaspoon chili powder, optional

2 tablespoons Ceylon curry powder (see page 12)

1/2 teaspoon whole fenugreek seeds

1 cinnamon stick

1 stem fresh lemon grass or 2 strips lemon rind

10 curry leaves

3 tablespoons vinegar

3 cups (24 fl oz, 750 ml) coconut cream

1 1/2 teaspoons ghee or oil for frying

Clean squid, removing ink sac and discarding head. Cut into rings. Put in a deep saucepan with all the ingredients except ghee. Bring to a boil, then simmer for about 1 hour or until squid is tender and the gravy reduced to a small quantity.

Drain pieces of squid from the gravy and, in another pan, heat the ghee and fry the squid. Pour the gravy into the pan in which the squid were fried, simmer for a minute or two longer and serve with white rice and sambols.

INDIA

# MADRAS SHRIMP CURRY

∾

SERVES: 6

2 lb (1 kg) raw shrimp (prawns)

1 tablespoon unsweetened desiccated coconut

1 tablespoon ground rice

2 cups (16 fl oz, 500 ml) coconut cream

2 tablespoons ghee or oil

12 curry leaves

2 medium onions, finely chopped

2 1/2 teaspoons finely chopped garlic

3 teaspoons finely grated fresh ginger

2 tablespoons Madras curry powder (see page 14) or Madras curry paste (see page 12)

1 teaspoon chili powder, optional

2 teaspoons paprika

1 1/2 teaspoons salt

2 tablespoons lemon juice

Shell and devein shrimps. Put desiccated coconut into a dry pan and toast over medium heat, shaking pan or stirring constantly until coconut is golden brown. Remove from pan and do the same with the ground rice. Put both into a blender with about 1/2 cup (4 fl oz, 125 ml) of the coconut cream and blend until smooth and coconut is very finely ground.

Heat ghee in a saucepan and fry the curry leaves for 1 minute. Add onions, garlic, and ginger and fry until golden brown, stirring with a wooden spoon. Add curry powder, chili powder, and paprika and fry on low heat, stirring. Do not let the spices burn. Add blended mix, rest of coconut cream, and salt, stir while bringing to simmering point. Do not cover. Simmer gently for 15 minutes, stirring occasionally.

Add shrimp, stir to mix, simmer for further 10 to 15 minutes or until shrimp are cooked and gravy thick. Stir in lemon juice. Serve with rice.

*BURMA*

# SHRIMP CURRY WITH GRAVY

∾

*ONE OF MY FAVORITE WAYS OF COOKING SHRIMP. THE ADDITION OF GREEN HERBS AT THE END OF COOKING GIVES EXTRA FLAVOR. CHARMAINE.*

SERVES: 4

1 lb (500 g) shelled shrimp (prawns)
1 large onion
3 cloves garlic
1 teaspoon finely grated fresh ginger
$^1/_2$ teaspoon ground turmeric
$^1/_2$ teaspoon chili powder
3 tablespoons light sesame oil or corn oil
pinch each of ground cloves, ground cardamom, and ground fennel
1 large potato, diced
2 ripe tomatoes, chopped
$^1/_2$ cup (4 fl oz, 125 ml) thin coconut cream
$^1/_2$ cup (4 fl oz, 125 ml) thick coconut cream
1 tablespoon chopped cilantro (fresh coriander leaves)
2 tablespoons chopped scallions (spring onion) leaves
salt to taste

Devein shrimp, prepare and cook basic ingredients as described on page 18. Add ground cloves, cardamom, fennel, potato, and tomato and stir well. Cook for 10 minutes with lid on pan. Add thin coconut cream and gently simmer uncovered for 10 minutes. Then add shrimp and thick coconut cream and simmer, stirring frequently, until shrimp are cooked, about 5 minutes.

Add cilantro and cook a further 2 or 3 minutes, then remove from heat and stir in the scallion leaves. Taste and add more salt if required. Serve hot with white rice and accompaniments.

*SRI LANKA*

# SALT FISH & EGGPLANT CURRY

∾

*YOU MAY THINK THIS IS A STRANGE COMBINATION, BUT BELIEVE ME, IT IS SO TASTY THAT WHENEVER I VISIT MY OLD HOME IN SRI LANKA I ASK FOR THIS SPECIAL CURRY. CHARMAINE.*

SERVES: 6

8 oz (250 g) dried salted fish
2 medium eggplants (aubergines), about 1 lb (500 g)
1 teaspoon ground turmeric
1 teaspoon salt
12 large fresh sweet chilies
oil for frying
10 cloves garlic, peeled and left whole
1 large onion, finely sliced
3 cups (24 fl oz, 750 ml) coconut cream
3 tablespoons Ceylon curry powder (see page 12)
small stick cinnamon
walnut size piece of tamarind pulp
$^1/_4$ cup (2 fl oz, 60 ml) malt vinegar
$^1/_2$ teaspoon salt, or to taste
1–2 teaspoons sugar

Wash the dried fish, drain, then cut into 2 in (5 cm) pieces. Slice the eggplants thickly, rub each slice with turmeric and salt and set aside for 30 minutes. Wash chilies, slit and remove seeds. Drain liquid that has come from eggplant slices and dry each slice with paper towels.

Heat about $^1/_4$ cup (2 fl oz, 60 ml) oil in a frying pan and fry separately the dried fish, eggplant, chilies, garlic, and onion removing each to a dish as fried. It may be necessary to replenish the oil as it is used up, for the eggplant absorbs quite a lot.

Put the coconut cream into a saucepan with the curry powder and cinnamon, tamarind dissolved in vinegar, and salt. Stir until it comes to a boil, add fried ingredients and keep stirring frequently as it cooks, uncovered. When it is thick, add sugar and stir to dissolve before serving.

*Note:* Sweet chilies are slightly wider in shape and milder in taste than hot chilies. They are popular with Indian cooks.

*CAMBODIA*

# SHRIMP & SWEET GOURD CURRY

∾

SERVES: 6

500g (1 lb) large raw shrimp (prawns)
1 sweet gourd or tender marrow or
2 green cucumbers
5 cloves garlic
1 small onion, roughly chopped
2 teaspoons finely chopped fresh ginger
$^1/_2$ teaspoon chili powder
$^1/_2$ teaspoon ground fennel
2 teaspoons ground coriander
$^1/_4$ teaspoon ground turmeric
4 tablespoons oil
2 cups (16 fl oz, 500 ml) coconut cream
1 stem lemon grass, bruised
2 tablespoons lemon juice
1 teaspoon sugar, optional
1 tablespoon fish sauce (see Glossary)

Shell and devein shrimp. Peel gourd or cucumbers, cut in halves lengthwise, scoop out seeds and cut in thick slices. Put garlic, onion, and ginger into an electric blender and blend to a purée. Mix in the ground spices.

Heat oil in a pan and fry the blended ingredients until they are well cooked and the oil starts to show around the edges, much as described in the basic method for Burmese curries (see page 18). Add the shrimp and stir fry for 3 minutes, then add coconut cream and bring to simmering point. Add sliced gourd or cucumber, remaining seasonings, and stir gently until vegetables are cooked and tender but not too soft. Serve with rice.

*INDIA*

# SHRIMP COCONUT CREAM CURRY

∾

SERVES 4

$1^1/_2$ lb (750 g) large raw shrimp (prawns)
1 tablespoon ghee or oil
2 medium onions, thinly sliced
1 teaspoon finely chopped garlic
1 teaspoon finely grated fresh ginger
2 fresh red or green chilies, slit and seeded
1 teaspoon ground turmeric
8 curry leaves
2 cups (16 fl oz, 500 ml) coconut cream
1 teaspoon salt
lemon juice to taste

Wash shrimp well. Shell and devein if liked, but Indian cooks say the shrimp should be in their shells, for they are tastier this way. Heat ghee and fry the onions, garlic, and ginger until onions are soft but do not let them brown. Add chilies, turmeric, and curry leaves and fry 1 minute longer. Add coconut cream and salt and stir while bringing to simmering point.

Simmer uncovered for 10 minutes, then add shrimp and cook for 10 minutes. Remove from heat and add lemon juice to taste.

BURMA

# SHRIMP CURRY, DRY

~

*A VERY EASY CURRY, BUT ONE OF THE MOST DELICIOUS. DON'T NEGLECT THE FRESH HERBS ADDED LAST OF ALL. REUBEN.*

SERVES: 4

1 lb (500 g) shelled shrimp (prawns)
1 large onion
3-4 cloves garlic
1 teaspoon finely grated fresh ginger
$^1/_2$ teaspoon ground turmeric
$^1/_4$ teaspoon chili powder
3 tablespoons light sesame oil or corn oil
1 tablespoon cilantro (fresh coriander leaves)
1 teaspoon salt or to taste
2 tablespoons chopped scallion (spring onion) leaves

Devein shrimp, rinse and drain. Prepare and cook basic ingredients as on page 18. When well cooked and sizzling, put in the shrimp and stir well. Sprinkle with the cilantro, cover and cook 3 or 4 minutes or until shrimp are done. Turn off heat, stir in the scallion leaves and serve hot with white rice and accompaniments.

MALAYSIA

# DRIED SHRIMP CURRY

~

SERVES: 3–4

250 g (8 oz) dried shrimp (prawns)
1 large onion, roughly chopped
2 teaspoons chopped garlic
8 dried red chilies, soaked
5 candlenuts or Brazil nuts, roughly chopped
2 teaspoons dried shrimp paste
1 teaspoon laos powder
3 tablespoons oil
1 stem lemon grass, finely chopped or rind of half lemon
$^1/_4$ cup (2 oz, 60g) tamarind liquid
1 teaspoon salt
$^3/_4$ cup (6 fl oz, 180 ml) thick coconut cream

Soak shrimp in hot water for 1 hour, drain and set aside. Put onion, garlic, dried chilies, nuts, dried shrimp paste, and laos powder in blender and blend to a smooth paste, adding a little hot water to facilitate blending.

Heat saucepan, add oil and when hot add lemon grass. Stir in the blended spices and cook until it smells fragrant and oil comes to the surface. Add the drained shrimp and cook a further 10 minutes on low heat, stirring occasionally. Add tamarind liquid and salt and cook for a further 5 minutes. Stir in coconut cream and serve with rice.

## INDIA

# SHRIMP CURRY

∽

SERVES: 4

1 lb (500 g) raw shrimp (prawns)
4–6 dry red chilies
$^1$/2 teaspoon cumin seeds
$^1$/4 teaspoon ground black pepper
1$^1$/2 teaspoons chopped garlic
1 teaspoon finely chopped fresh ginger
1 teaspoon ground turmeric
3 tablespoons oil
2 medium onions, chopped
1 ripe tomato, chopped
1 teaspoon salt
2 tablespoons vinegar

Shell and devein shrimp, rinse well and drain in colander. Discard seeds and stalks of chilies, and soak chilies in hot water for 5 minutes. Put chilies, cumin, pepper, garlic, ginger, and turmeric into blender and blend at high speed, adding a little oil to facilitate blending. If a blender is not available, substitute 2 teaspoons chili powder for dry chilies, ground cumin for cumin seeds, and finely grate the garlic and ginger. Mix these ingredients together with the turmeric.

Heat oil and fry onions until soft and golden. Add blended mixture and fry for a few minutes, then add the tomato, salt, and vinegar. Cover and cook until tomato is reduced to pulp. Add shrimp, stir well, cover and cook until shrimp are done, about 10 minutes. Serve with white rice.

## SRI LANKA

# RED SHRIMP CURRY

∽

*SRI LANKAN CURRIES ARE VERY HOT AND IN THIS RECIPE PAPRIKA IS SUBSTITUTED FOR PART OF THE CHILI TO GIVE THE RIGHT COLOR WITHOUT TOO MUCH HEAT. CHARMAINE.*

SERVES: 6

750 g (1$^1$/2 lb) small raw shrimp (prawns)
1 medium onion, finely chopped
1$^1$/2 teaspoons finely chopped garlic
1 teaspoon finely grated fresh ginger
small stick cinnamon
$^1$/4 teaspoon fenugreek seeds
few curry leaves
small stem lemon grass, bruised, or
2 strips lemon rind
1 strip daun pandan (rampé) leaf
$^1$/2 teaspoon ground turmeric
1$^1$/2 teaspoons chili powder
2 teaspoons paprika
1 teaspoon salt
2 cups (16 fl oz, 500 ml) coconut cream
good squeeze lemon juice

Wash shrimp and remove heads, but leave shells on. (In Sri Lanka shrimp are often cooked in their shells for better flavor.) Put all ingredients, except lemon juice, into a saucepan and bring slowly to simmering point. Simmer uncovered for 20 minutes or until onions are soft. Add lemon juice and stir. Taste and add more salt or lemon if required. Serve with rice, vegetable curries, and a sambol.

*MALAYSIA*

# SHRIMP CURRY

∾

SERVES 4

1 lb (500 g) large fresh shrimp (prawns)
1 large onion, roughly chopped
6 dried red chilies
2 fresh red chilies
2 teaspoons chopped garlic
1 teaspoon laos powder
1 teaspoon dried shrimp paste
1 teaspoon ground turmeric
2 tablespoons peanut oil
2 tablespoons lemon juice
1 tablespoon sugar
1 teaspoon salt

GARNISH
2 tablespoons chopped cilantro (coriander leaves)

Wash shrimp but do not remove heads and shells. Put onion, dried and fresh chilies, garlic, laos powder, dried shrimp paste, and turmeric in blender and blend to a paste on high speed, using a little water to facilitate blending.

Heat oil in a saucepan and fry the ground spices until they start to smell fragrant. Stir in the lemon juice, sugar, and salt, add the shrimp and stir till they turn red. Cover and simmer for 5 minutes, garnish with chopped cilantro and serve with rice.

See picture overleaf from page 114.

*THAILAND*

# SHRIMP RED CURRY

∾

SERVES: 4

1 lb (500 g) raw shrimp (prawns)
2 cups (16 fl oz, 500 ml) coconut cream (milk)
2 tablespoons red curry paste (see page 16)
1-2 tablespoons fish sauce (see Glossary) or
1 teaspoon salt
1 fresh red chili, seeded

Shell and devein shrimp, but reserve heads. Wash shrimp heads well, discarding only the hard top shell. Put the coconut cream into a pan with the curry paste, fish sauce, and the fresh chili. Bring slowly to simmering point, stirring. Add shrimp and shrimp heads and cook uncovered, stirring frequently, on low heat until shrimp are cooked and the taste has mellowed, about 15 minutes.

This curry is even better prepared ahead and reheated when required. Serve hot with white rice and other accompaniments. The shrimp heads are delicious and may be served as part of the curry.

# SHRIMP VINDALOO

∽

*USE STAINLESS STEEL OR ENAMEL PANS, ESPECIALLY FOR ACID CURRIES LIKE THIS ONE. IN ASIA SUCH DISHES ARE COOKED IN EARTHENWARE POTS. CHARMAINE.*

SERVES: 4

1 lb (500 g) large raw shrimp (prawns)
2 medium onions, roughly chopped
2 teaspoons chopped garlic
2 fresh red or green chilies, chopped
2 teaspoons chopped fresh ginger
$1/4$ cup (2 fl oz, 60 ml) white vinegar
$1^1/2$ teaspoons ground cumin
1 teaspoon garam masala
1 teaspoon ground turmeric
1 teaspoon salt
4 tablespoons oil
1 large onion, finely sliced
3 tablespoons lemon juice

Shell and devein shrimp, wash and drain well. Rub half the turmeric and salt over the shrimp. Put chopped onion, garlic, chilies, ginger, and vinegar in blender and grind to a pulp. If blender is not available crush the garlic, grate ginger finely and chop onions very fine. Add ground cumin and garam masala, remaining turmeric, and salt.

Heat oil in a saucepan and fry the chopped onion until soft and turning brown. Add the blended mixture and fry, stirring, until it is well cooked and oil separates from the mass. Add the shrimp, bring to a slow simmer and cook for 8 to 10 minutes. Stir in lemon juice and serve with rice.

# CRAB CURRY

∽

*WE TASTED THIS AT THE FORT AGUADA BEACH RESORT IN GOA. WHAT A BEAUTIFUL PLACE AND WHAT A BEAUTIFUL MEAL. REUBEN.*

SERVES: 4–6

2 or 3 medium size crabs
3 tablespoons oil or ghee
2 medium onions, finely chopped
2 teaspoons finely grated garlic
2 teaspoons finely grated fresh ginger
2 fresh red chilies, seeded and sliced
2 teaspoons ground coriander
2 teaspoons ground cumin
2 tablespoons ground almonds or white poppy seeds
2 bay leaves (tej pattar)
$1^1/2$ teaspoons salt or to taste
1 cup (12 fl oz, 250 ml) tomato purée
$1^1/2$ cups (12 fl oz, 375 ml) coconut cream
3 tablespoons chopped cilantro
(fresh coriander leaves)

Remove large shells of crabs and discard all fibrous tissue from under the shell. Divide each crab into 4 portions, breaking the body in half and separating the large, meaty claws from the body. Legs should be left attached to the body.

Heat the oil in a large saucepan and fry the onions, garlic, ginger, and chilies until onions are soft and golden. Add coriander, cumin, and ground almonds and fry for a minute or so longer. Then add the bay leaves, salt, tomato purée, and coconut cream and stir while bringing to a gentle simmer.

Put in the crabs and cook, uncovered, for 15 to 20 minutes or until the crabs are done. If pan is not large enough, cook in two lots. When cooked the shells will turn bright red and the flesh becomes white and opaque. If cooked crabs are used. reduce cooking time by half. Add cilantro during last 5 minutes. Serve with plain boiled rice.

*SRI LANKA*

# CRAB CURRY

∾

*A VERY SPECIAL DISH THAT IS USUALLY SERVED ONLY WITH PLAIN
WHITE RICE, NOTHING ELSE TO DISTRACT FROM THE SUPERB
FLAVOR OF THE CRAB AND THE SPICY SAUCE. CHARMAINE.*

SERVES: 4–6

2 large crabs

3 medium onions, roughly chopped

6 cloves garlic

2 teaspoons finely grated fresh ginger

$^1/_2$ teaspoon fenugreek seeds

10 curry leaves

3 in (8 cm) stick cinnamon

1-2 teaspoons chili powder

1 teaspoon ground turmeric

3 teaspoons salt

4 cups (32 fl oz, 1 l) thin coconut cream (milk)

2 tablespoons unsweetened, desiccated coconut

1 tablespoon ground rice

2 cups (16 fl oz, 500 ml) thick coconut cream

3 tablespoons lemon juice

Remove large shells of crabs and discard fibrous
tissue found under the shell. Divide each crab
into 4 portions, breaking each body in half and
separating large claws from body. Leave legs
attached to body.

Purée onion, garlic, and ginger in electric
blender. Heat oil in large saucepan and fry purée,
stirring for about 10 minutes. Add fenugreek,
curry leaves, cinnamon, chili powder, turmeric,
salt, and thin coconut cream. Cover and simmer
gently 30 minutes. Add crabs and cook for 20 minutes if using raw crabs. Cook for only 5 to 7 minutes if cooked crabs are used. If pan is not large
enough, simmer half the pieces of crab at a time.
Crab should be submerged in sauce while cooking.

Heat desiccated coconut and ground rice
separately in a dry frying pan over moderate
heat, stirring constantly to prevent burning,
until each is golden brown. Put in an electric
blender container, add half the thick coconut
cream, cover and blend on high speed 1 minute.
Add to curry with lemon juice. Wash out
blender with remaining coconut cream and add.
Simmer uncovered a further 10 minutes. Serve
with boiled rice.

See picture opposite page 114.

# POULTRY

CHICKENS ARE THE most popular birds in Asian cooking, followed by ducks, snipe, guinea fowl, teal, and paddy birds. Turkeys too make an occasional appearance, but goose is rarer than peafowl.

All are delicious when curried and sometimes I have referred to cutting the bird in 'curry pieces'. This means cutting pieces smaller than merely jointing, and enables the flavors to penetrate the meat readily.

To cut a chicken for curry, first joint the bird, then with a heavy cleaver cut each thigh in two. The breast is divided down the middle and each half cut into two. Wings are divided in two pieces, the first joint which looks like a small drumstick is detached from the breast, then the second joint and wing tip are separated from the first joint. Though the bony back of the bird is cut into three or four pieces and cooked with the curry for flavor, it is not counted as a serving piece because there is very little meat on the back except for the two "oysters" of flesh just above the thigh joint. Liver and giblets are also included in the curry, and indeed are so delicious that in the intimacy of family meals, they may be the bone of contention.

If the chicken weight is around 3 lb (1.5 kg), use the method described above. But if it is much smaller, the breast should only be divided into halves. On the other hand if it is much larger, even the drumsticks should be chopped in two.

Chicken is so versatile, it is equally delicious in gently spiced coconut cream curries, rich North Indian dishes and hot Sri Lankan, Malaysian, or South Indian curries, not to mention the numerous Indonesian dishes.

But when cooking duck, which has a stronger taste and richer meat, it is the hot, sour, vindaloo type of curry that suits it to perfection.

INDONESIA

# CHICKEN IN COCONUT CREAM

∾

*A WONDERFULLY FRAGRANT PREPARATION, SPICY BUT NOT HOT. A FINE INTRODUCTION TO CURRIES. CHARMAINE.*

SERVES: 4–6

1.5 kg (3 lb) roasting chicken or chicken pieces
1¹/₂ teaspoons finely grated garlic
1 teaspoon salt
¹/₂ teaspoon ground black pepper
1¹/₂ teaspoons finely grated fresh ginger
3 candle nuts or Brazil nuts, finely grated
3 teaspoons ground coriander
1 teaspoon ground cumin
¹/₂ teaspoon ground fennel
¹/₂ teaspoon laos powder, optional
4 tablespoons oil
2 medium onions, finely chopped
2 cups (16 fl oz, 500 ml) thin coconut cream
2 daun salam or 6 curry leaves
1 stem lemon grass or 3 strips thinly peeled lemon rind
5 cm (2 in) piece cinnamon stick
1¹/₂ cups (12 fl oz, 375 ml) thick coconut cream
1 tablespoon lemon juice or tamarind liquid (see Glossary)
extra salt to taste

Divide chicken into serving pieces. In a small bowl, combine garlic, salt, pepper, ginger, nuts, coriander, cumin, fennel, and laos powder if used. Mix to a paste, adding a little of the oil if necessary. Rub paste well into the pieces of chicken and leave for 1 hour.

Heat 2 tablespoons of the oil in a frying pan and fry sliced onion slowly until golden brown. Drain from oil and set aside. Add remaining oil to pan and fry the spiced chicken pieces gently, just until they start to yellow. Add thin coconut cream, daun salam, lemon grass or rind, and cinnamon stick. Stir until it comes to a boil, then cook uncovered for 30 minutes or until chicken is tender. Add thick coconut cream, stir thoroughly and cook for a further 15 minutes, uncovered. Remove from heat, add lemon juice and season to taste with extra salt. Remove whole spices. Garnish with fried onions and serve the chicken with white rice, vegetables, and sambals.

BURMA

# CHICKEN CURRY WITH SHRIMP PASTE

∾

*SHRIMP PASTE AND CHICKEN? GO AHEAD AND TRY IT — YOU'LL GO BACK FOR MORE. REUBEN.*

SERVES: 4–6

2 lb (1 kg) chicken, jointed
2 medium onions, sliced
2 tablespoons light sesame oil or corn oil
2 teaspoons dried shrimp paste
1 teaspoon finely chopped garlic
1 teaspoon finely chopped fresh ginger
1 teaspoon ground turmeric
1 teaspoon chili powder
2 teaspoons salt
¹/₂ cup (4 fl oz, 125 ml) hot water
squeeze of lemon juice

### GARNISH
¹/₄ cup (¹/₂ oz, 15g) chopped cilantro (fresh coriander)

Heat oil in a saucepan and brown onions on medium heat. Add shrimp paste, garlic, and ginger, lower heat and stir for a few minutes. Add turmeric, chili powder, and salt, stir well and cook 1 minute longer. Add chicken and mix till well coated. Add water and bring to a boil.

Turn heat low, cover and simmer until chicken is tender, stirring occasionally. Add lemon juice, sprinkle with chopped cilantro and serve with white rice.

SRI LANKA

# CHICKEN CURRY

∾

*YOUR SRI LANKAN GUESTS WILL SHAKE THEIR HEADS WITH JOYOUS APPROVAL IF YOU DRY ROAST THE CORIANDER, CUMIN, AND FENNEL TO A RICH BROWN BEFORE USING THEM IN THIS DISH. REUBEN.*

3 lb (1.5 kg) chicken or chicken pieces
3 tablespoons ghee or oil
1/4 teaspoon fenugreek seeds, optional
10 curry leaves
2 large onions, finely chopped
2–2 1/2 teaspoons finely chopped garlic
2 teaspoons finely grated fresh ginger
1 teaspoon ground turmeric
1 teaspoon chili powder
1 tablespoon ground coriander
1 teaspoon ground cumin
1/2 teaspoon ground fennel
2 teaspoons paprika
2 teaspoons salt
2 tablespoons vinegar
2 tomatoes, peeled and chopped
6 cardamom pods, bruised
1 stick cinnamon
1 stem fresh lemon grass or 2 strips lemon rind
1 cup (12 fl oz, 250 ml) thick coconut cream

Joint chicken. Cut breast and thighs in halves, leave wings and drumsticks whole. Heat ghee and fry fenugreek and curry leaves until they start to brown. Add onions, garlic, and ginger and fry gently until onions are quite soft and golden. Add turmeric, chili, coriander, cumin, fennel, paprika, salt, and vinegar. Stir well.

Add chicken and stir over medium heat until chicken is thoroughly coated with spices. Add tomatoes, whole spices, and lemon grass and cook, covered, over low heat 40 to 50 minutes. Add coconut cream, taste and add more salt and a squeeze of lemon juice if desired. Do not cover after adding coconut cream. Serve with rice and accompaniments.

*Note:* Paprika is used to give the required redness – in Sri Lanka the redness is achieved by using about 30 red chilies!

See picture opposite page 67.

INDIA

# MADRAS CHICKEN CURRY

∾

*BE WARNED. THIS IS A REALLY HOT CURRY. REMEMBER TO EAT IT WITH SUFFICIENT QUANTITIES OF RICE, AND KEEP THE BEER OR WATER WELL WITHIN REACH! REUBEN.*

SERVES: 6

3 lb (1.5 kg) roasting chicken
3 tablespoons oil
12 curry leaves
2 medium onions, finely chopped
2 teaspoons finely chopped garlic
2 teaspoons finely chopped fresh ginger
1 teaspoon ground turmeric
3 teaspoons chili powder
3 teaspoons ground coriander
1 teaspoon ground cumin
2 1/2 teaspoons salt
1 large, ripe tomato, peeled and chopped
2 small sticks cinnamon
2 cups (16 fl oz, 500 ml) coconut cream

Cut chicken into curry pieces (see page 62). Heat oil, fry curry leaves, onions, garlic, and ginger until soft. Add turmeric, chili powder, coriander, and cumin. Fry for 2 minutes. Add salt and tomato, stir well, cover and cook until tomato is pulpy. Add chicken and cinnamon sticks and stir well until chicken is coated with the spice mixture.

Cover and cook for 30 minutes, or until chicken is almost tender. Stir in the coconut cream and simmer, uncovered, for about 15 minutes longer. Serve with rice and accompaniments.

BURMA

# CHICKEN CURRY WITH GRAVY

∾

SERVES: 4–6

3 lb (1.5 kg) chicken
2 medium onions
3 cloves garlic
1 teaspoon finely grated fresh ginger
1 stem lemon grass or 2 strips lemon rind
3 tablespoons vegetable oil
2 teaspoons salt or to taste
1 teaspoon turmeric
1 teaspoon chili powder, optional
1 cup (12 fl oz, 250 ml) water
1 large ripe tomato, chopped
2 large potatoes, peeled and cubed or
2 cups (3¹/₂ oz, 100 g) cauliflower sprigs
1 tablespoon fish sauce (see Glossary)
1 tablespoon tamarind liquid (see Glossary)
or lemon juice
1 tablespoon chopped fresh cilantro (coriander leaves)
¹/₄ teaspoon ground cardamom

Proceed as for Chicken Curry, Dry (see page 67). When chicken is half-cooked, add water, tomato, potato, fish sauce, and tamarind or lemon juice. Continue cooking until potato is done, stirring occasionally. If cauliflower is used in preference to potato, add it when chicken is nearly done. Finally add cilantro and cardamom. Stir and serve.

*THAILAND*

# CHICKEN WITH COCONUT CREAM & LAOS

∾

*IN SOUTH-EAST ASIAN COUNTRIES, FRESH LAOS, AN AROMATIC RHIZOME, IS A POPULAR INGREDIENT. IN COUNTRIES WHERE IT DOES NOT GROW, A THUMB-SIZED PIECE OF LAOS IS REPLACED BY A FEW SLICES OF DRIED LAOS, OR THE EASIER-TO-USE LAOS POWDER. CHARMAINE.*

SERVES: 5

6 slices fresh or dried laos or 4 teaspoons
laos powder
1 roasting chicken, about 2¹/₂ lb (1.25 kg)
2¹/₂ cups (20 fl oz 600 ml) thin coconut
cream
¹/₂ teaspoon black pepper
2-3 fresh coriander roots, crushed
6 strips thinly peeled lemon rind
3 fresh green chilies
1¹/₂ teaspoons salt
3 fresh leaves from lemon or other citrus tree
1 cup (12 fl oz, 250 ml) thick coconut cream (milk)
1 tablespoon fish sauce (see Glossary)
lemon juice to taste
3 tablespoons finely chopped cilantro
(fresh coriander leaves)

Soak the dried laos in hot water for 30 minutes and pulverize in blender with some of the liquid. Cut chicken into serving pieces and put into saucepan with thin coconut cream, laos, pepper, coriander roots, lemon rind, chilies (whole), salt, and citrus leaves. Bring slowly to a boil and simmer, uncovered, until chicken is tender, stirring occasionally. Add thick coconut cream and stir constantly until it returns to a boil.

Remove from heat and stir in the fish sauce and lemon juice. Serve in a deep dish or bowl sprinkled with chopped cilantro and accompanied with white rice.

*INDIA*

# CHICKEN SHAGUTI

∾

SERVES: 6

3 lb (1.5 kg) roasting chicken
8 dried red chilies
1 tablespoon ground coriander
1 teaspoon ground cumin
$^1/_2$ teaspoon fenugreek seeds
8 whole black peppercorns
3 teaspoons white poppy seeds or ground almonds
$^1/_2$ cup (2 oz, 60 g) unsweetened desiccated coconut
1 large onion, finely sliced
2 teaspoons chopped fresh ginger
2 teaspoons chopped garlic
$^1/_2$ teaspoon ground cardamom
$^1/_4$ teaspoon ground cloves
$^1/_2$ teaspoon ground cinnamon
2 teaspoons salt
1 tablespoon ghee
2 tablespoons oil
1 teaspoon ground turmeric
juice of half a lemon

Cut chicken into curry pieces. Remove stalks and seeds from chilies and soak the chilies in hot water for 10 minutes. Meanwhile, roast coriander and cumin in a dry pan over medium heat for a minute or two, until they turn brown and a pleasant aroma is given off. Turn onto a plate. Roast fenugreek seeds and peppercorns for 2 or 3 minutes, stirring constantly or shaking pan. In the same way roast the poppy seeds and the desiccated coconut, separately. Add to the other roasted spices. Put the sliced onion in the pan and dry roast, stirring, until brown.

Put chilies into electric blender with all the roasted ingredients and the turmeric, cardamom, cloves, and cinnamon. Add some of the water in which the chilies were soaked and grind to a paste.

Heat ghee and oil in a heavy pan and fry the ground mixture and the ginger and garlic, stirring constantly, until oil separates from the mass. Put in the chicken, sprinkle with salt and stir to coat every piece of chicken with the spices.

Add $^1/_2$ cup (4 fl oz, 125 ml) hot water, cover and cook on very low heat, stirring occasionally and adding more water if necessary, until the chicken is tender. Add lemon juice when chicken is cooked. The gravy should be very thick and dark. Serve with rice and accompaniments, such as Onion and Tomato Sambal (page 91) and Beetroot Raita (page 95).

See picture opposite.

*INDONESIA*

# JAVANESE CHICKEN CURRY

∾

SERVES: 4–6

1 x 1.5 kg (3 lb) roasting chicken
1 medium onion, chopped
1 teaspoon finely chopped garlic
1 teaspoon chopped fresh ginger
3 fresh red chilies or 1 teaspoon sambal ulek
2 candle nuts or Brazil nuts
3/4 cup (6 fl oz) coconut cream
1 tablespoon desiccated or fresh grated coconut
2 teaspoons ground coriander
1 teaspoon laos powder, optional
$^1/_2$ teaspoon ground turmeric
1$^1/_2$ teaspoons salt
1 stem fresh lemon grass, or
3 strips thinly peeled lemon rind
2 daun salam or 6 curry leaves

Cut chicken into curry pieces (see page 62). Put onion, garlic, ginger, chilies, and nuts in blender container with half the coconut cream and the desiccated coconut. Cover and blend on high speed for approximately 30 seconds or until smooth. Rinse blender container with remaining coconut cream and add to pan. Add all remaining ingredients, and bring slowly to a boil, stirring. Cook, uncovered, until chicken is tender and gravy thick and almost dry.

Serve with white rice and a sayur (vegetable cooked in coconut cream) or a curry with plenty of gravy.

*Chicken Shaguti (page 66).*

*Chicken Curry (page 64).*

INDIA

# CHICKEN VINDALOO

∾

*THE VINEGAR AND SPICES USED IN THIS PREPARATION ALLOW THE CHICKEN TO BE KEPT FOR WEEKS — IF YOU CAN RESIST IT FOR SO LONG! REUBEN.*

SERVES: 6

4 lb (2 kg) roasting chicken
2 tablespoons cumin seed
1 tablespoon black mustard seed
3 teaspoons chili powder or to taste
1 tablespoon chopped ginger
1 tablespoon chopped garlic
3/4 cup (6 fl oz, 180 ml) vinegar
1 teaspoon ground cinnamon
1/4 teaspoon ground cloves
1/4 teaspoon ground cardamom
4 tablespoons oil
2 teaspoons salt
1/2 teaspoon ground black pepper

Cut the chicken into curry pieces (see page 62). Grind the cumin seeds, mustard seeds, ginger, and garlic in electric blender with the vinegar. Use high speed so that mixture is finely ground. Add the ground spices.

Heat oil in a heavy saucepan, remove from heat and add the ground mixture to the hot oil. Stir for a few seconds, then add the chicken pieces and stir again so that each piece is coated with the spices. Let it stand for an hour or longer. Return to low heat and bring to simmering point, add salt and black pepper and simmer, covered, until chicken is tender. Stir from time to time so that spices do not catch to the base of pan. Serve with plain white rice.

BURMA

# CHICKEN CURRY, DRY

∾

*THIS DRY CURRY IS USUALLY SERVED WITH A GARLIC-SHRIMP-BASED SOUP TO MOISTEN THE RICE. REUBEN.*

SERVES: 4–6

3 lb (1.5 kg) chicken
2 medium onions
3 cloves garlic
1 teaspoon finely grated fresh ginger
1 stem lemon grass or 2 strips lemon rind
3 tablespoons vegetable oil
1 1/2 teaspoons salt or to taste
1 teaspoon ground turmeric
1/2 teaspoon chili powder, optional
1/4 teaspoon ground cardamom
1 tablespoon chopped fresh cilantro (coriander leaves)

Cut chicken into curry pieces. Peel and roughly chop onions and put into blender container with garlic, ginger, sliced lemon grass or lemon rind. Add a little oil to facilitate blending and blend ingredients to a smooth pulp.

Heat remaining oil in a saucepan and when very hot add blended ingredients, salt, turmeric, and chili powder (if used) and fry over medium heat, stirring well with a wooden spoon. Add a few drops of water if mixture starts to catch to base of pan. Simmer on low heat until the moisture content of the onions has evaporated and the ingredients turn a rich red-brown. At this stage they will begin to catch to the pan so keep stirring, and add the chicken pieces, turning them well in the mixture so that they become well coated.

Cover and simmer for 35 to 45 minutes or until chicken is tender. The juices from the chicken will provide sufficient liquid for this curry, so do not add water or other liquid. As cooking is nearing completion, stir occasionally to prevent catching. Add cardamom and cilantro, stir quickly and replace lid for a few seconds to hold in the aroma. Serve with white rice and other accompaniments.

*MALAYSIA*

# CHICKEN CURRY WITH TOASTED COCONUT

~

SERVES: 6

3 lb (1.5 kg) roasting chicken

4-6 fresh red chilies

$^1/_2$ cup ($1^1/_2$ oz, 45 g) unsweetened desiccated coconut

2 cups (16 fl oz, 500 ml) thick coconut cream

2 onions, roughly chopped

3 cloves garlic

1 teaspoon dried shrimp paste

1 teaspoon ground turmeric

1 tablespoon ground coriander

2 teaspoons ground cumin

1 stem fresh lemon grass or 2 strips lemon rind

3 tablespoons peanut oil

2 teaspoons salt

4 daun salam or 6 curry leaves

2 teaspoons laos powder

Cut chicken into joints. Drain. Remove chili seeds if you don't want a very hot curry.

Put desiccated coconut into a heavy frying pan and fry on medium heat, stirring constantly, until it becomes dark brown. Immediately turn on to a plate, for it will burn if left in the pan. When cooled slightly put it into an electric blender. Grind finely. then add about half a cup (4 fl oz, 125 ml) of the coconut cream and blend again on high speed for 1 minute.

Set the coconut mixture aside in a bowl and, without washing blender container, put in the chilies, onions, garlic, dried shrimp paste, turmeric, coriander, cumin, and sliced lemon grass or lemon rind. Blend to a purée. The water content of the onions should be enough to turn the mixture to a purée but if necessary add a tablespoon of the peanut oil. Heat remaining oil in a large saucepan and fry the onion mixture on low heat, stirring constantly, until moisture evaporates and oil shows around edge. Add ground coconut,

coconut cream, salt, daun salam, and laos powder and stir well. Add chicken and stir gently as mixture comes to simmering point. Simmer, uncovered, for 1 hour or until chicken is tender, stirring occasionally. Serve with rice and other accompaniments.

*MALAYSIA*

# HOT CHICKEN CURRY

~

SERVES: 6

1.5 kg (3 lb) chicken, jointed

1 tablespoon ground coriander

1 teaspoon ground fennel

1 teaspoon ground black pepper

5 candle nuts or 4 Brazil kernels, chopped

8 dried red chilies

1 teaspoon chopped garlic

$^1/_2$ teaspoon ground turmeric

$^1/_2$ teaspoon ground cinnamon

1 stem fresh lemon grass, finely sliced or rind of half a lemon

1 teaspoon laos powder

2 teaspoons salt

3 tablespoons peanut oil

3 medium onions, finely sliced

3 fresh red chilies, sliced

hot water

$^1/_2$ cup (4 fl oz) coconut cream

Place in electric blender the coriander, fennel, pepper, chopped nuts, chilies, garlic, turmeric, cinnamon, lemon grass, laos, and salt. Blend to a fine paste, adding a little water.

Heat oil in a large saucepan and fry onions till soft and golden. Add blended mixture and cook stirring, till oil comes to the surface and mixture smells aromatic. Add chicken and sliced chilies and cook, stirring for 5 minutes. Lower heat and cook covered till chicken is tender, stirring occasionally, and adding a little hot water to prevent sticking. Stir in coconut cream, simmer further 5 minutes and serve with rice and accompaniments.

*INDIA*

# HUNDRED ALMOND CURRY

*SOUNDS EXTRAVAGANT? WELL, WHY NOT. WHO SHOULD COUNT PENNIES WHEN CREATING A MASTERPIECE? REUBEN.*

SERVES: 6

3$^1$/$_2$ lb (1.75 kg) roasting chicken
or 2 lb (1kg) boneless lamb
5 medium onions
2 tablespoons ghee
2 tablespoons oil
3 teaspoons finely chopped garlic
3 teaspoons finely grated fresh ginger
1 tablespoon ground coriander
1 tablespoon ground cumin
1 teaspoon ground turmeric
$^1$/$_2$ teaspoon ground fennel
1 teaspoon chili powder, optional
3 teaspoons salt
3 large ripe tomatoes, peeled and chopped
$^1$/$_4$ cup ($^1$/$_2$ oz, 15 g) chopped cilantro
(fresh coriander leaves) or mint leaves
100 blanched almonds about 4 oz (125 g)
oil for frying
1 cup (12 fl oz, 250 ml) natural yogurt
1 teaspoon garam masala (see page 12)

Cut chicken into curry pieces or lamb into large cubes. Peel onions, chop 3 onions finely and slice the remaining two very fine. Heat ghee and oil in a large heavy saucepan and fry the sliced onion, stirring, until it is golden brown. Remove from pan and set aside. Add the chopped onion, garlic, and ginger to the oil left in pan and fry on low heat, stirring occasionally, until very soft and turning golden. Long, slow cooking at this stage is essential if the curry is to have a good rich taste.

Add the coriander, cumin, turmeric, fennel, and chili powder and fry, stirring, for a minute or two. Add salt, tomatoes, and half the fresh herbs, stir well and cook until tomatoes are pulpy. Cover pan to hasten this process, but uncover and stir now and then to ensure mixture does not catch to base of pan.

Put in the chicken pieces and stir well. Cover pan and cook on very low heat for 40 minutes or until chicken is tender. Meanwhile, heat oil and fry half the almonds until golden. In electric blender grind remaining almonds. Beat the yogurt with a fork until it is quite smooth and stir into the curry together with the fried almonds. Simmer 5 minutes, uncovered. Stir in the garam masala, reserved fried onions, ground almonds, and remaining chopped herbs. Heat through and serve.

*INDIA*

# CURRIED CHICKEN LIVERS

SERVES: 4–5

1 lb (500 g) chicken livers
2 tablespoons ghee or oil
2 medium onions, finely chopped
1 teaspoon finely grated garlic
2 teaspoons finely grated fresh ginger
$^1$/$_2$ teaspoon ground turmeric
$^1$/$_2$ teaspoon chili powder
1 tablespoon ground coriander
2 teaspoons ground cumin
2 ripe tomatoes, peeled and chopped
1 teaspoon salt
1 teaspoon garam masala

Wash the livers and drain in a colander. Cut them in halves and if there are any yellow spots on the livers slice them off with a sharp knife. Heat the ghee or oil in a heavy saucepan and fry the onion, stirring occasionally, until soft. Add the garlic and ginger and continue frying until golden.

Add turmeric, chili powder, coriander, and cumin. Fry for 2 minutes, stirring, then add the tomatoes and salt and cook, covered, on low heat until tomatoes are puréed, stirring occasionally. Add the chicken livers and stir gently. Replace lid and cook for 15 minutes, sprinkle garam masala over and simmer for a minute or two. Serve hot with rice and other accompaniments.

*BURMA*

# CHICKEN CURRY WITH NOODLES

∽

*SERVE NOODLES IN A LARGE BOWL AND THE CURRY IN A SEPARATE BOWL. EACH PERSON TAKES A SERVING OF NOODLES, LADLES ON A GENEROUS AMOUNT OF THE CURRY AND SPRINKLES VARIOUS ACCOMPANIMENTS OVER THE TOP. CHARMAINE.*

SERVES: 6–8

3 lb (1.5 kg) chicken or chicken pieces
5 cloves garlic
3 medium onions, chopped
1 tablespoon finely chopped fresh ginger
1 teaspoon dried shrimp paste
2 tablespoons peanut oil
1 tablespoon sesame oil
1-2 teaspoons chili powder
2 teaspoons salt
2 cups (16 fl oz, 500 ml) thin coconut cream
2 cups (16 fl oz, 500 ml) thick coconut cream
2 tablespoons chickpea flour
1 lb (500 g) thin egg noodles or cellophane noodles

Cut chicken into serving pieces. Put garlic, onion, ginger, and dried shrimp paste into blender container, cover and blend until smooth, adding 1 tablespoon of peanut oil if necessary. Heat remaining oil and fry blended ingredients for 5 minutes. Add chicken and continue to fry, stirring constantly. Add chili powder, salt, and thin coconut cream. Simmer until chicken is tender, adding a little hot water if mixture becomes too dry.

Add thick coconut cream, return to heat and bring slowly to a boil, stirring constantly to prevent mixture from curdling. Mix chickpea flour with a little cold water to a smooth cream, add to curry and cook for a further 5 minutes uncovered (there should be a lot of gravy). If preparing curry a day or two beforehand, refrigerate immediately and reheat when required.

Just before serving, cook noodles in a large saucepan of boiling salted water until just tender, about 6 minutes. Pour cold water into pan to stop noodles cooking, then drain in colander.

ACCOMPANIMENTS:

finely sliced spring onions, both green and white portions
chopped fresh cilantro (coriander leaves)
finely sliced white onion
roasted chick peas, finely ground in a blender or crushed with mortar and pestle
crisp fried noodles, broken into small pieces
fried onion flakes
thin slices garlic, fried in oil until golden
lemon wedges
dried chilies, fried in oil 3-4 seconds
chili powder

*Note:* Roasted chick peas are sold in Greek delicatessen shops.

See picture opposite page 35.

*THAILAND*

# GREEN CURRY OF CHICKEN

∽

Proceed as for Green Curry of Duck (page 74) but substitute 1 large roasting chicken.
See picture opposite page 82.

MALAYSIA

# CHICKEN & BAMBOO SHOOT CURRY

∾

*THE CONTRASTING TEXTURES OF BAMBOO SHOOT AND CHICKEN PRODUCE A VERY UNUSUAL CURRY. CHARMAINE.*

SERVES: 6–8

1 x 1.5 kg (3 lb) roasting chicken
1 can bamboo shoots
2 medium onions
4 tablespoons coconut or peanut oil
1$^1$/$_2$ tablespoons ground coriander
1 teaspoon dried shrimp paste
1 teaspoon laos powder
1 teaspoon chili powder
2 teaspoons salt
2 cups (16 fl oz, 500 ml) thin coconut cream
1 cup (12 fl oz, 250 ml) thick coconut cream

Cut chicken into curry pieces. Drain bamboo shoots and cut into quarters, then into slices. Chop onions finely. Heat the oil in a large saucepan and fry onions over medium heat, stirring, until soft and golden. Add coriander, dried shrimp paste, laos, chili powder, and salt and fry, stirring constantly, for a few minutes until spices are brown.

Add chicken pieces and stir until well mixed with the spices, then add thin coconut cream and bring to simmering point. Simmer for 20–25 minutes. Add bamboo shoot, stir, and simmer for a further 20 minutes or until chicken is tender. Add thick coconut cream and simmer, uncovered, stirring gently. Taste and add salt if necessary. Continue simmering until oil rises to the surface. Serve with rice, vegetables and sambal.

SRI LANKA

# CHICKEN WHITE CURRY

∾

*FRESH DILL SEEMS SO SCANDINAVIAN, BUT IT IS A POPULAR HERB IN CERTAIN DISHES IN SRI LANKA. TRY IT ALSO IN MEATBALLS AND FISH CAKES. CHARMAINE.*

SERVES: 4–6

1.5 kg (3 lb) chicken, jointed
1 tablespoon chopped fresh dill weed
1 teaspoon chopped garlic
1 teaspoon chopped fresh ginger
$^1$/$_2$ teaspoon ground turmeric
2 teaspoons salt
2 teaspoons chili powder
1 tablespoon ground coriander
1 teaspoon ground cumin
$^1$/$_2$ teaspoon ground fennel
$^1$/$_4$ teaspoon fenugreek seeds
1 stick cinnamon
2 stems fresh lemon grass, bruised
12 curry leaves
2 medium onions, finely sliced
2 cups (16 fl oz, 500 ml) thick coconut cream
hot water
1 tablespoon ghee or oil
2 teaspoons black mustard seeds

Place chicken in a saucepan with dill weed, garlic, ginger, turmeric, salt, chili powder, coriander, cumin, fennel, fenugreek, cinnamon, and lemon grass. Also add half the curry leaves, one sliced onion, half the coconut cream and sufficient hot water to cover the chicken pieces. Bring to a rapid boil, lower heat, cover and simmer for 20 minutes, stirring occasionally.

In another saucepan heat the ghee, add the remaining curry leaves, remaining sliced onion and mustard seeds. Stir-fry till onions are soft and golden, then stir in remaining coconut cream. Add this mixture to saucepan containing the chicken, stir well and cook further 10 minutes or until chicken is tender. Serve with rice and accompaniments.

SRI LANKA

# CHICKEN GIZZARD CURRY

∾

*IF YOU HAVEN'T HAD CURRIED GIBLETS BEFORE, WHY NOT? IT'S THE 'IN' THING. REUBEN.*

SERVES: 6

750 g (1$^1$/$_2$ lb) chicken gizzards
1$^1$/$_2$ tablespoons ground coriander
3 teaspoons ground cumin
4 tablespoons oil or ghee
2 medium onions, finely chopped
2$^1$/$_2$ teaspoons finely chopped garlic
1 tablespoon finely chopped fresh ginger
1 teaspoon chili powder
$^1$/$_2$ teaspoon ground turmeric
$^1$/$_2$ teaspoon ground fenugreek, optional
2 ripe tomatoes, chopped
1$^1$/$_2$ teaspoons salt
2 tablespoons chopped fresh cilantro (coriander leaves)

Wash and clean the gizzards well, leave to drain in colander. Put the ground coriander in a small dry pan and stir over low heat for a few minutes until roasted to a fairly dark brown and spreading a pleasant aroma. Turn the coriander on to a plate. Roast the cumin in the same way.

Heat the oil in a large heavy saucepan. When hot, put in onions, garlic, and ginger. Fry, stirring, until onions are soft and start to turn golden brown. Add the chili powder, turmeric, fenugreek, and the previously roasted coriander and cumin. Cook, stirring, for 1 minute, then add the tomatoes and salt and stir well. Add the chicken gizzards and stir until they are well coated with spice mixture. Add hot water to cover and simmer for 1 hour or until gizzards are tender. Sprinkle with cilantro (coriander leaves), stir and cook for 5 minutes longer. Serve hot with rice.

THAILAND

# MOSLEM CHICKEN CURRY

∾

SERVES: 6–8

1 roasting chicken about 1.75 kg (3$^1$/$_2$ lb)
4 cups (32 fl oz, 1 L) coconut cream (milk)
1 cup (5 oz) roasted, unsalted peanuts
2 tablespoons fish sauce
15 cardamom pods
1 stick cinnamon, about 5 cm (2 in)
1 quantity Moslem curry paste (see page 17)
3 tablespoons tamarind liquid
2 tablespoons lime or lemon juice
1–2 tablespoons sugar
extra fish sauce if necessary

Cut chicken into curry pieces (see page 62). Put into a saucepan with the coconut cream, peanuts, fish sauce, cardamom pods, and cinnamon. Bring slowly to simmering point, stirring frequently with a wooden spoon. Turn heat low and allow to simmer, uncovered, until meat is tender. This should take about 35-40 minutes. Do not cover at any stage or the coconut cream will curdle. Stir occasionally during this initial cooking.

Meanwhile, make the curry paste. When the chicken is just tender lift it out and simmer the coconut cream a little longer, until it is reduced by about a third. If it has already reduced considerably, do not give it this further cooking. Stir in the curry paste, tamarind liquid, lemon juice, and sugar. Return chicken to pan and continue simmering until the gravy is thickened slightly. Taste and add more fish sauce if necessary. Serve with white rice.

# CHICKEN & YOGURT CURRY

~

*THE TANGY FLAVOR OF THE YOGURT BLENDS WITH AND
COMPLEMENTS THE SPICES USED IN THIS RECIPE. REUBEN.*

SERVES: 4

1 kg (2 lb) roasting chicken
1 medium onion, roughly chopped
3 cloves garlic, peeled
1 teaspoon finely chopped fresh ginger
$^1/_2$ cup (2 oz) fresh coriander or mint leaves
$1^1/_2$ tablespoons ghee or oil
1 teaspoon ground turmeric
$1^1/_2$ teaspoons garam masala (see page 12)
$1^1/_2$ teaspoons salt
$^1/_2$ teaspoon chili powder, optional
$^1/_2$ cup (4 fl oz) natural yogurt
2 ripe tomatoes, diced

GARNISH
extra chopped mint or cilantro
(coriander leaves).

Cut chicken into serving pieces, or use chicken
pieces of one kind – drumsticks, thighs or half
breasts.

Put into container of electric blender the
onion, garlic, ginger, fresh coriander or mint.
Blend to a smooth purée. Heat oil in a heavy
saucepan and fry the blended mixture, stirring,
for about 5 minutes. Add turmeric, garam
masala, salt, and chili powder and fry for a
further minute. Stir in yogurt and tomatoes, and
fry until liquid dries up and the mixture is the
consistency of thick purée.

Add chicken pieces, turning them in the spice
mixture so they are coated on both sides, then
turn heat low, cover tightly and cook until chick-
en is tender. If liquid from chicken has not evaporated by the time the flesh is cooked, uncover
and raise heat to dry off excess liquid, stirring
gently at the base of pan to prevent burning.
Garnish with chopped herbs and serve with rice
or chapatis.

# CHICKEN DOPIAZA

~

SERVES: 6

1 x 1.5 kg (3 lb) roasting chicken
6 medium onions
4 fresh green chilies, seeded
4 teaspoons chopped garlic
$1^1/_2$ tablespoons finely grated fresh ginger
1 tablespoon ground coriander
1 tablespoon ground cumin
2 teaspoons ground turmeric
1 teaspoon ground cinnamon
1 tablespoon ground cardamom
$^1/_2$ teaspoon ground cloves
6 tablespoons ghee or oil
3 ripe tomatoes, peeled and chopped
3 teaspoons salt
1 cup (12 fl oz, 250 ml) water

Cut chicken into curry pieces. Thinly slice half the
onions and set aside. Roughly chop the rest of the
onions and put into container of electric blender
with the chilies, garlic, and ginger. Blend to a
purée. Mix in the ground spices, coriander, cumin,
turmeric, cinnamon, cardamom, and cloves.

Heat ghee or oil in a large saucepan and fry
the sliced onions, stirring frequently, until they
are golden brown. Remove onions from pan with
slotted spoon. Add the ground mixture to oil
remaining in pan and fry, stirring, until color
darkens and oil appears around the edges. Add
tomatoes, stir and cook until liquid from tomatoes is almost evaporated. Add the chicken pieces
and stir well. Add water and salt, cover and cook
for 35 minutes or until chicken is tender. Add
reserved fried onions, cover and simmer 5 minutes longer. Serve with rice or parathas.

# GREEN CURRY OF DUCK

∾

*THE GREEN COLOR IS IMPARTED BY THE FINELY CHOPPED CHILIES AND FRESH HERBS ADDED DURING THE LAST FEW MINUTES OF COOKING. THESE TWO INGREDIENTS GIVE COLOR, BUT ALSO A DISTINCTIVE FLAVOR THAT DISTINGUISHES THAI DISHES FROM OTHER SPICED PREPARATIONS WITH A COCONUT CREAM GRAVY. PLEASE NOTE THAT CANNED COCONUT CREAM CANNOT BE USED IN THIS RECIPE.*

SERVES: 4

1 roasting duck, 1.5 kg (3 lb)
$3^{1}/_{2}$–4 cups (28–32 fl oz) coconut cream
3 tablespoons green curry paste (see page 13)
2 sprigs tender citrus leaves
1 teaspoon salt
2 tablespoons fish sauce
2 tablespoons finely chopped fresh green chilies, seeds removed
4 tablespoons finely chopped fresh basil or cilantro (coriander leaves)

Divide duck into joints. Make coconut cream as instructed on page 8 and put the first extract or thick milk in the refrigerator or in a cool place for an hour or so until the cream rises to the top. Spoon off the cream or richest part of the milk into a cup. Heat this cupful of coconut cream in a large heavy saucepan, stirring constantly until it comes to a boil. Lower heat and continue cooking, stirring occasionally, until the cream thickens and oil bubbles around it. By this time it should be reduced to a quarter of the original amount. Add the curry paste and fry the rich oily cream for about 5 minutes, stirring constantly. The curry paste will smell cooked and oil will separate from it when it is ready.

When this happens add the pieces of duck and cook over medium low heat stirring frequently and turning them, for about 15 minutes. The duck will change color and have a cooked appearance. Add the remaining coconut cream, citrus leaves, salt, and fish sauce and stir while the coconut cream comes to a boil. Then turn heat low and allow to simmer uncovered for 35–45 minutes or until the duck is well cooked and tender and the gravy rich and oily. (In Thai curries, the aim is not to reduce the liquid to a small amount of thick, almost dry curry, so add extra coconut cream if necessary.) Stir in the chopped fresh chilies and herbs, simmer for 5 minutes longer, then turn into serving dish. Serve with white rice.

# DUCK CURRY, DRY

∾

*THIS IS A VERY RICH CURRY THAT SHOULD BE OFFSET BY PLAIN WHITE RICE AND OTHER LIGHTER CURRIES SUCH AS A WHITE VEGETABLE CURRY. PIQUANT ACCOMPANIMENTS SUCH AS PICKLED LIME SAMBOL AND A FRESH CUCUMBER AND ONION SALAD ALSO GO WELL WITH IT. CHARMAINE*

SERVES: 4–5

1.5 kg (3 lb) duck, jointed
2 large onions, chopped
3 teaspoons chopped garlic
$1^{1}/_{2}$ tablespoons finely chopped fresh ginger
2 tablespoons Ceylon curry powder (see page 12)
1 stick cinnamon
8 strips rampé leaf (pandanus)
1 stem fresh lemon grass or rind of half a lemon
3 cups (24 fl oz) coconut cream
2 teaspoons salt
$^{1}/_{4}$ cup (2 fl oz, 60 ml) vinegar
1 tablespoon brown sugar
2 tablespoons ghee or oil

Joint duck and place into a large heavy saucepan with all the ingredients except sugar and ghee. Bring to a boil, then cover and simmer until duck is tender.

Heat ghee in another pan and fry the pieces of duck, then pour in the gravy, add sugar and simmer a further 10 minutes. Serve with rice and accompaniments.

*MALAYSIA*

# DUCK CURRY, DRY

∼

SERVES: 4–5

1.5 kg (3 lb) duck, jointed
3 medium onions, roughly chopped
5 candle nuts or 4 Brazil kernels, chopped
6 dried red chilies
$^1/_2$ teaspoon turmeric
1 teaspoon dried shrimp paste
1 teaspoon ground cardamom
$^1/_2$ teaspoon ground cinnamon
$^1/_2$ teaspoon ground cloves
1 teaspoon laos powder
2 teaspoons salt
3 tablespoons peanut oil
1 tablespoon curry leaves
$^1/_4$ cup (2 fl oz, 60 ml) coconut cream
hot water

Place in container of electric blender the onions, Brazil kernels, chilies, turmeric, dried shrimp paste, cardamom, cinnamon, cloves, laos, and salt. Blend to a fine paste, adding a little water to facilitate blending.

Heat oil in a large saucepan. Add curry leaves and the blended mixture and cook, stirring, till oil comes to the surface and the mixture smells aromatic. Stir in the duck pieces and cook for 5 minutes. Lower heat and simmer covered till duck is tender, stirring occasionally, and adding a little hot water to prevent catching. Stir in coconut cream and cook uncovered till gravy thickens. Serve with rice and accompaniments.

*INDONESIA*

# PADANG DUCK CURRY

∼

SERVES: 4–5

1.5 kg (3 lb) duck, jointed
3 daun salam or 6 curry leaves
2 cups (16 fl oz, 500 ml) thick coconut cream
3 medium onions, roughly chopped
1 teaspoon laos powder
2 teaspoons chopped garlic
1 teaspoon chopped fresh ginger
$^1/_2$ teaspoon dried shrimp paste
1 teaspoon ground turmeric
4 dried red chilies
1 stem fresh lemon grass, finely sliced or rind of $^1/_2$ lemon
5 candle nuts or 4 Brazil kernels, chopped
2 teaspoons salt
2 teaspoons tamarind paste
$^1/_2$ cup hot water

Place in container of electric blender the onions, laos, garlic, ginger, shrimp paste, turmeric, chilies, lemon grass, and candlenut kernels. Blend to a fine paste, adding a little hot water to facilitate blending.

Put duck, daun salam and coconut cream in a saucepan, add blended ingredients and bring to a boil. Add the salt and tamarind paste dissolved in hot water, reduce heat and simmer, stirring frequently, until coconut cream is absorbed and the oil comes to the surface. Add sufficient hot water to prevent catching, stir and cook until duck is tender. Serve with rice.

## INDIA
# DUCK VINDALOO
∾

*I WOULD USE THE CHILI SEEDS FOR A REALLY HOT, TANGY DISH.
REUBEN.*

*I WOULD REMOVE THE SEEDS UNLESS COOKING FOR CONFIRMED
CHILI FREAKS. CHARMAINE.*

SERVES: 4–5

1 x 1.5 kg (3 lb) duck
10 dried red chilies
$^1/_2$ cup (4 fl oz) vinegar
1 tablespoon chopped garlic
1 tablespoon chopped fresh ginger
1 tablespoon ground coriander
2 teaspoons ground cumin
1 teaspoon ground turmeric
$^1/_2$ teaspoon ground black pepper
2–3 tablespoons ghee or oil
2 teaspoons salt
1 tablespoon sugar

Cut the duck into joints. Remove stalks and seeds from dried chilies and soak in vinegar for about 10 minutes. Put chilies, vinegar, garlic, and ginger into container of electric blender and blend until smooth. Scrape mixture out of blender into a large bowl and mix in the ground spices. Add pieces of duck, turn them over in the mixture until they are well coated, cover and leave for 2 hours at room temperature or overnight in the refrigerator.

In a large saucepan heat the ghee or oil and fry the pieces of duck lightly. Add salt and a little hot water together with any marinade left. Cover and simmer on low heat until duck is tender, adding a little more water if necessary during cooking. At end of cooking time stir in the sugar. Serve with rice.

## SRI LANKA
# OMELET CURRY
∾

SERVES: 4

OMELETS
6 eggs
1 small onion, finely chopped
1 fresh green chili, seeded and finely chopped
2 teaspoons fresh dill, finely chopped
or $^1/_2$ teaspoon dried dill weed
salt and pepper to taste
ghee or butter

GRAVY
3 cups (24 fl oz) thin coconut cream
1 medium onion, finely sliced
2 fresh chilies, seeded and split
$^1/_2$ teaspoon ground turmeric
1 teaspoon finely sliced garlic
$^1/_2$ teaspoon finely grated fresh ginger
1 stick cinnamon
4 dried rampé leaves
2 stems fresh lemon grass, bruised
8 curry leaves
salt to taste
1 cup (12 fl oz, 250 ml) thick coconut cream

*Omelets:* Beat eggs together, add onion, chili, dill, salt,. and pepper. Heat a little ghee in a frying pan and make 2 omelets with mixture. Cut each omelet in 3 pieces. Heat through in prepared gravy and serve with boiled rice and accompaniments.

*Gravy:* Place all ingredients, except thick coconut cream, in a large saucepan and simmer gently, uncovered, for approximately 10 minutes. Add thick coconut cream, stir and simmer 5 minutes longer.

INDIA

# EGG CURRY

∾

*SO YOU CAN'T HANDLE A HOT CURRY? TRY THIS —*
*SANS CHILI POWDER. REUBEN.*

SERVES: 4–6

6 eggs
2 tablespoons ghee or oil
2 medium onions, finely chopped
$1^1/2$ teaspoons finely chopped garlic
2 teaspoons finely grated fresh ginger
3 teaspoons ground coriander
2 teaspoons ground cumin
1 teaspoon ground turmeric
$^1/2$ teaspoon chili powder
2-3 ripe tomatoes, diced
1 teaspoon salt or to taste
$^1/2$ cup hot water
$^1/2$ teaspoon garam masala (see page 12)

Hard boil the eggs, cool quickly under running cold tap, then shell and set aside. Heat ghee or oil and fry onions, garlic, and ginger until soft and golden brown. Add coriander, cumin, turmeric and chili and fry for a few seconds, then add tomatoes and salt and stir over medium heat until tomatoes are soft and pulpy.

Add hot water, cover and simmer until gravy is thick, then stir in garam masala and the halved eggs and heat through. Serve with rice.

SRI LANKA

# RABBIT CURRY

∾

*VENISON, PEAFOWL, HARE, SNIPE, TEAL ARE THE GAME AVAILABLE*
*IN SRI LANKA, BUT I SUGGEST RABBIT IN PLACE OF THESE*
*MORE EXOTIC CREATURES. THEY ALSO MAKE A SIMILAR CURRY*
*USING IGUANA WHICH, I AM TOLD, COULD BE MISTAKEN FOR*
*CHICKEN. NO, I HAVEN'T TASTED IT AND I HOPE I NEVER DO!*
*CHARMAINE.*

*I HAVE, IT'S GREAT! REUBEN.*

1.5 kg (3 lb) rabbit, jointed
1 tablespoon ground coriander
1 teaspoon ground cumin
1 teaspoon ground fennel
8 dried red chilies
1 large onion, roughly chopped
2 teaspoons chopped garlic
2 teaspoons chopped fresh ginger
1 teaspoon ground turmeric
1 stem fresh lemon grass, chopped or rind of half lemon
1 teaspoon ground cardamom
1 teaspoon ground cinnamon
$^1/2$ teaspoon ground cloves
2 teaspoons salt
2 tablespoons vinegar
hot water
1 cup (12 fl oz, 250 ml) thick coconut cream
8 curry leaves
1 tablespoon ghee or oil

Dry roast coriander, cumin, and fennel to a golden brown. Place in the container of electric blender with the chilies, onion, garlic, ginger, turmeric, lemon grass, cardamom, cinnamon, cloves, salt, and vinegar. Blend to a smooth paste, adding a little hot water to facilitate blending.

Place rabbit pieces in a saucepan, add the blended mixture, coconut cream and sufficient hot water to cover. Bring to a fast boil, lower heat and simmer until rabbit is tender and the gravy reduced.

In another saucepan heat the ghee, add the curry leaves and rabbit pieces. Stir fry for 2 minutes then add the gravy to it. Serve with rice and accompaniments.

# VEGETABLES

MANY MILLIONS OF Asians live on a pure vegetarian diet. This is especially true in India. In this chapter there are therefore many recipes from India, where fresh vegetables are combined with dried beans or lentils, or with fresh home-made cheese. This is the protein that balances the Indian diet.

In Asia, vegetables are never boiled in water and the water thrown away – that would be looked upon as foolishness, as indeed it is. Judiciously spiced and seasoned, vegetables are made so delicious that they could be relished as the only accompaniment to rice and chapatis even by those who are not totally vegetarian.

Use the recipes in this section as a guide, then adapt them to whatever vegetables are in season and create interesting combinations of your own.

## INDIA
# BEAN & CABBAGE FOOGATH

∽

*THIS IS CHARMAINE'S. SHE HAS A TOUCH OF MAGIC WITH VEGETABLES. REUBEN.*

SERVES: 6

250 g (8 oz) green beans
half a small cabbage
4 tablespoons oil
1 large onion, finely chopped
2 fresh green chilies, sliced (optional)
1 teaspoon finely chopped fresh ginger
1 teaspoon ground turmeric
1¹/₂ teaspoons salt, or to taste
3 tablespoons desiccated coconut

Top and tail beans and cut into diagonal slices. Finely shred the cabbage. In a large saucepan heat oil and fry the onion, chilies, and ginger until golden. Add turmeric, then toss in the vegetables and mix over low heat until vegetables are tender but still crisp. Sprinkle salt, mix well. Add coconut and toss over heat until any liquid is absorbed. Serve with rice or chapatis.

## INDIA
# CAULIFLOWER CURRY

∽

*THIS IS A GOOD EXAMPLE OF A 'DRY CURRY' AND THE MUNDANE CAULIFLOWER NEVER TASTED SO GOOD. CHARMAINE*

SERVES: 4–6

half a large cauliflower
4 tablespoons oil
1 teaspoon black mustard seeds
1 onion, finely chopped
1 teaspoon finely chopped garlic
1 teaspoon finely chopped fresh ginger
1 teaspoon ground turmeric
¹/₂ teaspoon chili powder, optional
1¹/₂ teaspoons salt or to taste

Separate cauliflower into sprigs, leaving some of the stalk on each. Heat the oil in a karhai (or wok) or large saucepan and fry the mustard seeds until they pop. Add the onion, garlic, and ginger and fry until soft. Add turmeric, chili powder, and salt and stir well, then toss the cauliflower in the mixture so that all the pieces are tinged with yellow. Add ¹/₂ cup (4 fl oz) water, cover pan and simmer for 10–15 minutes or until cauliflower is tender but not mushy. Taste and add more salt if necessary and serve with rice.

*INDONESIA*

# BEAN SAYUR

∾

SERVES: 6

2 tablespoons peanut oil
1 onion, finely chopped
1 teaspoon finely chopped garlic
2 fresh red chilies, seeded and chopped
1 teaspoon dried shrimp paste
1 teaspoon finely grated lemon rind
2 teaspoons ground coriander
1 teaspoon ground cumin
$^1/_2$ teaspoon laos powder
1 teaspoon salt
2 tablespoons tamarind liquid or lemon juice
1 daun salam or 3 curry leaves
3 cups chicken stock
1 lb (500 g) fresh green beans, sliced
1 cooked chicken breast, skinned, boned and diced
$1^1/_2$ cups (12 fl oz, 375 ml) coconut cream

Heat oil, fry onion, garlic, chilies, and dried shrimp paste for 5 minutes over medium heat, stirring and crushing shrimp paste with back of spoon. Add lemon rind and ground spices, fry 1 minute. Add salt, tamarind liquid, daun salam or curry leaves stock, and beans. Bring to a boil, simmer for 8 minutes. Add chicken and coconut cream. Simmer 5 minutes and serve.

Note: Rice vermicelli can be added to this sayur when it is the main dish. Soak 125 g (4 oz) of rice vermicelli in very hot water for 10 minutes, and drain well. Add to sayur and cook for further 2 minutes.

See picture opposite page 83.

*NEPAL*

# NEPALESE PEA & POTATO CURRY

∾

SERVES: 4

3 tablespoons ghee and oil mixture
1 large onion, finely sliced
$^1/_2$ teaspoon ground black pepper
3 green chilies, chopped
2 teaspoons finely chopped garlic
1 teaspoon finely chopped fresh ginger
$^1/_2$ teaspoon ground turmeric
1 teaspoon salt, or to taste
1 lb (500 g) potatoes, peeled and cubed
2 cups fresh green peas
2 large tomatoes, chopped
2 teaspoons ground coriander
1 teaspoon toasted ground cumin
1 cup (12 fl oz, 250 ml) hot water

GARNISH
2 tablespoons fresh cilantro (coriander leaves), chopped

Heat ghee and oil mixture in a saucepan and fry onion till soft and golden. Stir in pepper, chilies, garlic, ginger, turmeric, and salt. Continue cooking for 2 or 3 minutes then add potatoes and stir till light brown all over.

Add remaining ingredients and hot water, stir well, cover and simmer till vegetables are tender and the oil shows on the surface. Garnish with chopped cilantro (coriander leaves) and serve with chapatis or rice, and accompaniments.

SRI LANKA

# YELLOW PUMPKIN CURRY

∾

*A MILD, SLIGHTLY SWEET CURRY THAT APPEALS TO CHILDREN AND ADULTS ALIKE. CHARMAINE.*

SERVES: 6

1 lb (500 g) pumpkin
1 small onion, finely chopped
1 teaspoon finely chopped garlic
3 fresh green chilies, seeded and chopped
8–10 curry leaves
$1/2$ teaspoon fenugreek seeds
$1/2$ teaspoon ground turmeric
2 teaspoons pounded Maldive fish
or dried shrimp (prawns)
$1^1/2$ cups (12 fl oz, 375 ml) thin coconut cream
1 teaspoon salt
cup (4 fl oz) thick coconut cream
1 teaspoon black mustard seeds

Peel pumpkin and cut into large chunks. Put into a pan with all the ingredients except the thick coconut cream and mustard seeds. Bring slowly to simmering point and cook gently, uncovered, until pumpkin is almost tender.

Meanwhile, grind the mustard seeds in mortar and pestle and mix with the thick coconut cream. Add to the simmering pot and cook for 5 minutes longer on a very gentle heat.

BURMA

# LONG BEANS & TOMATO CURRY

∾

*WHEN LONG BEANS ARE NOT IN SEASON, SUBSTITUTE THE EASILY OBTAINED FRENCH BEANS. CHARMAINE.*

SERVES: 2–3

250 g (8 oz) long beans,
chopped into 3.75 cm ($1^1/2$ in) lengths
2 tablespoons peanut oil
6 curry leaves
1 medium onion, finely sliced
1 teaspoon dried shrimp paste
$1/2$ teaspoon salt
$1/2$ teaspoon ground black pepper
1 teaspoon chili powder
1 large tomato, finely chopped
2 teaspoons finely chopped garlic
$1/2$ cup hot water
1 teaspoon sesame oil

Heat oil in a saucepan, add curry leaves then add onion and stir till soft and golden. Add dried shrimp paste, salt, pepper, chili, tomato, and garlic. Stir well for 2 minutes, add water, lower heat, cover and simmer until oil comes to the surface.

Raise heat and stir in the beans for 1 minute. Cover and simmer till cooked, crunchy but not mushy. Add sesame oil, stir and serve with rice and accompaniments.

# FRESH PEANUT CURRY

∾

SERVES: 2–4

250 g (¹/₂ lb) shelled raw peanuts
¹/₂ cup (1¹/₂ oz) desiccated coconut
2 teaspoons finely chopped garlic
1 tablespoon ground coriander
1¹/₂ teaspoon ground turmeric
¹/₂ teaspoon ground chili powder
3 tablespoons oil
2 medium onions, finely sliced 1
tomato, peeled and chopped
1 teaspoon sugar, or to taste
1¹/₂ teaspoons salt
hot water
¹/₂ teaspoon garam masala

GARNISH
2 tablespoons chopped fresh cilantro
(coriander leaves)

Soak peanuts in water for 2 hours, then boil for 20 minutes. Drain and set aside. Place coconut, garlic, coriander, turmeric, and chili powder in container of electric blender with enough water to allow blades to move freely. Blend to a paste on high speed, remove contents and set aside.

Heat oil and fry onions till soft and golden. Add tomato and the blended mixture and cook, stirring, until it smells fragrant and the oil comes to the surface.

Add nuts, sugar, salt, and 1 cup hot water. Bring to a boil, cover and simmer for 15 minutes or until peanuts are cooked. Sprinkle with garam masala and garnish with chopped cilantro (coriander leaves). Serve with hot rice and accompaniments.

# POTATO CURRY

∾

*FOR ALL IRISH CURRY LOVERS! REUBEN.*

SERVES: 3–4

1 lb (500 g) potatoes
1 tablespoon ghee
1 tablespoon oil
¹/₂ teaspoon black cumin seeds
¹/₂ teaspoon black mustard seeds
1 onion, finely chopped
2 teaspoons finely grated ginger
1 teaspoon ground turmeric
1 teaspoon ground cumin
¹/₂ teaspoon chili powder
1¹/₂ teaspoons salt
1 cup (12 fl oz, 250 ml) hot water
1 teaspoon garam masala
2 tablespoons lemon juice

GARNISH
2 tablespoons finely chopped fresh mint or fresh
coriander

Peel potatoes and cut into large cubes. Heat the ghee and oil in a heavy saucepan with a well-fitting lid and fry the black cumin and mustard seeds until they pop. Add onion and ginger and fry, stirring, until soft and golden. Add the turmeric, ground cumin, and chili powder, stir quickly, add the salt and the potatoes and toss all together well.

Add hot water to pan, cover and cook on very low heat for 20 minutes. Sprinkle garam masala and lemon juice over, shake pan with lid on, allow to cook for a further 5 to 10 minutes, until potatoes are cooked. Serve garnished with chopped herbs.

*Green Curry of Chicken (page 70).*

*Bean Sayur (page 80).*

INDONESIA

# Spicy Cabbage in Coconut Cream

∾

*THIS IS CALLED A 'SAYUR' IN INDONESIA, AND A SIMILAR DISH IS CALLED 'WHITE CURRY' IN SRI LANKA AND 'MOLEE' IN INDIA. SERVE WITH RICE ALONGSIDE ONE OF THE DRIER TYPES OF MEAT CURRIES. CHARMAINE.*

SERVES: 4

1 lb (500 g) cabbage
2 onions, chopped
2 cloves garlic
2 fresh red chilies, seeded and chopped, or 1 teaspoon chili powder
1 teaspoon dried shrimp paste
1 daun salam or 3 curry leaves
2 tablespoons peanut oil
2 strips lemon rind
1 1/2 cups thick coconut cream
1 teaspoon salt
3 tablespoons tamarind liquid (see Glossary)

Wash and coarsely shred the cabbage. Put chopped onions, garlic, and chilies into container of electric blender and blend to a purée. Or grate onions and garlic, and chop chilies finely or substitute chili powder. Wrap the shrimp paste in a piece of foil and roast under the broiler (grill) for 5 minutes, turning halfway through.

In a wok or large saucepan fry the daun salam or curry leaves in hot oil for 1 minute, turn in the blended mixture and the shrimp paste and fry, stirring, until the mixture turns a darker color. Stir constantly or mixture might catch to base of pan. Add lemon rind, coconut cream, and salt, stir well while bringing to simmering point. Add the cabbage and simmer, uncovered, for a few minutes until the cabbage is cooked but still crisp. Stir in the tamarind liquid and serve.

INDIA

# Mushroom & Potato Curry

∾

*THIS IS THE KIND OF DISH THAT COULD TURN ME INTO A VEGETARIAN. SMALL NEW POTATOES CUT IN HALVES MAY BE USED INSTEAD OF DICED LARGE POTATOES FOR A CHANGE IN APPEARANCE AND TEXTURE. CHARMAINE.*

SERVES: 4–6

375 g (12 oz) button mushrooms, whole
250 g (8 oz) potatoes, diced
3 tablespoons peanut oil
1 teaspoon dried fenugreek leaves
1 large onion, finely chopped
2 teaspoons finely chopped garlic
1 teaspoon finely chopped fresh ginger
1 large tomato, chopped
2 tablespoons chopped fresh cilantro (coriander leaves)
1 teaspoon chili powder
1 teaspoon ground turmeric
1 teaspoon salt, or to taste
1/2 cup hot water
1/2 teaspoon garam masala

Heat oil in a saucepan, add fenugreek leaves, then onion and fry till soft and golden. Stir in garlic, ginger, tomatoes, and cilantro (coriander leaves) and cook, stirring, for 2 minutes. Add chili powder, turmeric, salt, and hot water. Bring to a boil then stir in mushrooms and diced potatoes.

Cover and simmer, stirring occasionally, until potatoes are tender. Sprinkle with garam masala and serve with Indian bread or rice and accompaniments.

*INDIA*

# CURRIED DRIED BEANS

∾

*ANY OF THE DRIED BEANS MAY BE USED FOR THIS CURRY. I PARTICULARLY FAVOR CHICK PEAS. REUBEN.*

SERVES: 4

250 g (8 oz) dried beans
water
2 teaspoons salt
1 1/2 tablespoons ghee or oil
1 large onion, finely chopped
1 teaspoon finely chopped garlic
1 tablespoon finely chopped fresh ginger
1 teaspoon ground turmeric
1 teaspoon garam masala (see page 12)
2 large ripe tomatoes, chopped
1–2 fresh green chilies, seeded and chopped
2 tablespoons chopped fresh mint
2 tablespoons lemon juice

Soak dried beans in plenty of cold water overnight. Drain, rinse and put beans into a large saucepan with water to cover and 1 teaspoon salt. Bring to a boil, cover and cook until tender. Add more hot water during cooking if necessary. Drain and reserve cooking liquid.

Heat ghee in large saucepan and gently fry the onion, garlic, and ginger until soft and golden, then add turmeric, garam masala, tomatoes, chilies, mint, remaining teaspoon salt, and lemon juice. Add the beans and stir well over medium heat for 5 minutes. Add 1 cup (12 fl oz, 250 ml) reserved liquid, cover and cook over low heat until tomatoes and chilies are soft and the gravy thick. Serve with rice or Indian breads as part of a vegetarian meal.

*SRI LANKA*

# VEGETABLE CURRY

∾

*HERE IS THE BASIC WHITE CURRY. IN IT YOU CAN COOK BEANS, PUMPKIN, OKRA, CAPSICUM, POTATOES, ZUCCHINI, ASPARAGUS, OR OTHER VEGETABLES OF YOUR CHOICE. CHARMAINE.*

SERVES: 4–6

3 cups (24 fl oz) thin coconut cream (milk)
1 medium onion, finely sliced
2 fresh green chilies seeded and split
1/2 teaspoon ground turmeric
1 teaspoon finely chopped garlic
1/2 teaspoon finely grated fresh ginger
5 cm (2 in) cinnamon stick
4 pieces dried daun pandan leaf (rampé)
1 stem lemon grass or 2 strips lemon rind, optional
8 curry leaves 750 g (1 1/2 lb) vegetables, sliced
salt to taste
1 cup (12 fl oz, 250 ml) thick coconut cream

Put all ingredients, except sliced vegetables, salt, and thick coconut cream, in a large saucepan and simmer gently, uncovered, for approximately 10 minutes.

Add sliced vegetables and salt and cook gently until vegetables are just tender. Add thick coconut cream and simmer about 5 minutes longer. Serve with boiled rice and accompaniments.

# CASHEW NUT CURRY

∾

*A CURRY OF FRESH CASHEW NUTS IS ONE OF THE DELIGHTS OF SINHALESE COOKING. FRESH CASHEW NUTS ARE NOT OBTAINABLE EXCEPT IN THE COUNTRY IN WHICH THEY ARE GROWN, BUT RAW CASHEWS, FROM HEALTH FOOD SHOPS AND CHINESE GROCERY STORES, MAKE A VERY GOOD SUBSTITUTE IF SOAKED OVERNIGHT IN COLD WATER. CHARMAINE.*

Proceed as for vegetable curry (see opposite), but substitute 250 g (8 oz) raw cashew nuts for sliced vegetables. Simmer for approximately 30 minutes, or until cashews are tender. Serve with boiled rice and other accompaniments.

# VEGETABLE CURRY

∾

SERVES: 6 AS AN ACCOMPANIMENT

1 onion, finely sliced
$^1/_2$ teaspoon finely chopped garlic
2 fresh red or green chilies, seeded and sliced
$^1/_2$ teaspoon dried shrimp paste
$^1/_2$ teaspoon ground turmeric
1 cup (12 fl oz, 250 ml) thin coconut cream
1 large potato, peeled and diced
3 cups coarsely shredded cabbage
1 teaspoon salt
1 cup (12 fl oz, 250 ml) thick coconut cream
lemon juice to taste

Put the onion, garlic, chilies, dried shrimp paste, turmeric and thin coconut cream into a saucepan and bring to simmering point. Add potato and cook for 10 minutes or until potato is half cooked.

Add cabbage and salt, cook for 3 minutes, then add the thick coconut cream and stir gently until cabbage is cooked. Remove from heat and add lemon juice to taste.

# BROWN LENTIL & TOMATO CURRY

∾

SERVES: 4

1 cup brown lentils
2 teaspoons ghee
2 tablespoons peanut oil
1 medium onion, thinly sliced
3 tablespoons chopped cilantro (coriander leaves)
2 medium tomatoes, chopped
2 teaspoons finely chopped garlic
1 teaspoon finely chopped fresh ginger
2 teaspoons ground cumin
1 teaspoon chili powder
1 teaspoon turmeric
salt to taste
1 tablespoon lemon juice
$^1/_2$ teaspoon garam masala

Soak lentils for 2 hours and boil in 4 cups (32 fl oz, 1 L) water till cooked but still firm. Drain and set aside. Heat ghee and oil and fry onion till soft and golden. Stir in chopped coriander, tomatoes, garlic, ginger, and cumin and cook further 3–4 minutes.

Add chili powder, turmeric, salt, and lemon juice and cook till mixture smells aromatic, stirring occasionally. Add lentils, mix thoroughly and cook further 4 minutes. Sprinkle with garam masala and serve with chapatis or rice, and accompaniments.

INDIA

# MOGHUL VEGETABLE CURRY

∾

*I ARGUED THAT REUBEN WAS BEING HEAVY-HANDED WITH THE SPICES BUT WHEN I TASTED THE RESULT I HAD TO ADMIT HE HAD A WINNER. CHARMAINE.*

4 cups diced mixed vegetables
(carrots, potatoes, beans, peas)
1/4 cup (3 oz) blanched almonds
6 cloves
2 teaspoons cardamom seeds
1 teaspoon dried fenugreek leaves
5 cm (2 in) cinnamon stick, broken
2 teaspoons chopped garlic
1/2 teaspoon chili powder
1/2 teaspoon ground turmeric
hot water
3 tablespoons ghee
1 large onion, finely sliced
1/4 teaspoon ground saffron
1/2 cup (4 fl oz) natural yogurt
salt to taste
1/2 cup (4 fl oz) water

Place almonds, cloves, cardamom, fenugreek leaves, cinnamon, garlic, chili powder, and turmeric in container of electric blender with enough hot water to enable blades to move freely. Blend to a paste on high speed, remove contents and set aside.

Heat ghee in a saucepan and fry onion till soft and golden. Stir in the paste and fry till it smells fragrant and ghee comes to the surface. Add saffron powder and stir in mixed vegetables and yogurt. Add salt and water and bring to a boil, cover and simmer till vegetables are tender. Serve with Indian bread and accompaniments.

INDIA

# SPINACH & CHEESE CURRY

∾

*THIS IS REUBEN'S SPECIALITY. HE SIMPLY LOVES THE FLAVOR OF FENUGREEK LEAVES AND IF I DON'T WATCH HIM HE WILL PUT THEM IN JUST ABOUT EVERYTHING. CHARMAINE.*

SERVES: 2–4

1 bunch spinach, leaves only
250 g (8 oz) ricotta cheese, cubed
oil for frying
2 teaspoons dried fenugreek leaves
1 large onion, finely sliced
2 teaspoons finely chopped garlic
1 teaspoon finely chopped fresh ginger
2 teaspoons ground cumin
1/2 teaspoon ground turmeric
1 medium tomato, chopped
1 teaspoon salt
juice of half lemon

Boil spinach in 1 cup (12 fl oz, 250 ml) water for 5 minutes, drain, chop and set aside. Fry cheese cubes to a golden brown and set aside.

Heat 3 tablespoons oil in a saucepan, stir in fenugreek leaves then onion and fry till soft and golden. Stir in garlic, ginger, cumin, turmeric, tomato, salt, and lemon juice. Cook till oil comes to the surface and the mixture smells fragrant.

Mix in the spinach and cook for a further 5 minutes. Gently stir in the cheese cubes, heat through and serve with rice and accompaniments.

*BURMA*

# PUMPKIN & COCONUT CURRY

~

*THIS IS A SOUPY CURRY AND IS QUITE A FAVORITE IN BURMA. REUBEN.*

SERVES: 2–4

1 lb (500 g) pumpkin, peeled and cubed
1 large onion, finely sliced
2 teaspoons finely chopped garlic
1 teaspoon turmeric
1 teaspoon chili powder
1 teaspoon salt
$^1/_2$ teaspoon ground black pepper
1 teaspoon dried shrimp paste
2 tablespoons creamed coconut or $^1/_2$ cup thick coconut cream
$1^1/_2$ cups (12 fl oz, 375 ml) hot water
2 fresh green chilies, sliced

Place all ingredients, except pumpkin, into a saucepan and bring to a boil. Lower heat and simmer for 5 minutes. Add pumpkin, cover and simmer until tender. Serve with rice and accompaniments.

*INDIA*

# LENTIL PURÉE

~

SERVES: 4–5

250 g (8 oz) red lentils
2 tablespoons ghee or oil
1 onion, finely sliced
2 cloves garlic, sliced
1 teaspoon finely chopped fresh ginger
$^1/_2$ teaspoon ground turmeric
3 cups (24 fl oz) hot water
1 teaspoon salt, or to taste
$^1/_2$ teaspoon garam masala, optional

Wash lentils, discarding those that float. Drain well. In a saucepan heat ghee or oil and fry onion, garlic, and ginger until golden. Add turmeric and

stir for a few seconds, then add the drained lentils and fry for a minute. Add hot water and bring to a boil, reduce heat, cover and simmer until lentils are soft before adding salt and garam masala. Continue cooking until the consistency of porridge.

*INDIA*

# BENGAL EGGPLANT CURRY

~

*THE MUSTARD OIL IMPARTS QUITE A DISTINCTIVE FLAVOR, BUT IF YOU CANNOT BUY IT EASILY SUBSTITUTE PEANUT OIL. REUBEN.*

SERVES: 4

2 tablespoons each of mustard oil and peanut oil
1 teaspoon mustard seeds
1 teaspoon fenugreek seeds
$^1/_2$ teaspoon fennel seeds
1 large onion, finely sliced
1 large eggplant, cubed
1 teaspoon finely chopped garlic
2 teaspoons ground coriander
1 teaspoon ground cumin
1 teaspoon chili powder
2 whole bay leaves
$^1/_2$ teaspoon turmeric
1 cup fresh green peas
1 teaspoon salt, or to taste
1 tablespoon vinegar
1 cup hot water

Heat oils in a saucepan and fry mustard, fenugreek and fennel seeds till mustard seeds start to pop, then add onion and fry till soft and golden. Stir in the cubed eggplant and continue to fry a further 5 minutes.

Add the rest of the ingredients and stir well for 2 more minutes. Stir in hot water, bring to a boil, cover, and simmer till vegetables are cooked but not mushy. Serve with hot rice and accompaniments.

# ACCOMPANIMENTS

IN ANY CURRY meal, it is those titillating morsels like chutneys, pickles, pappadams, sambals, and so on that complement the main dishes, providing accents of flavor and texture which make a good curry meal so memorable. The creative cook will allow imagination free rein in this area, adding to the menu accompaniments which give a stamp of individuality.

While most of the recipes for accompaniments may be served with the main dishes of another country's cuisine, it appears that the strong garlic and shrimp flavors of some Burmese and Thai accompaniments are only at home with Burmese and Thai foods. They may even be served with some Malaysian or Indonesian dishes, but are completely at variance with Indian flavors. So while you can mix and match main dishes of one country with sambals and salads from another, be discriminating enough to keep strong flavors from dominating a gently spiced meal.

*THAILAND*

# CHILI SALAD
~

10 fresh green chilies, chopped
1 tablespoon shrimp powder
2 teaspoons grated garlic
1–2 tablespoons fish sauce
3 teaspoons finely chopped lemon rind
juice of half a lemon

Mix all ingredients together and serve with curry and boiled rice.

*INDIA*

# FRESH MINT CHUTNEY
~

*IN ADDITION TO ITS REFRESHING FLAVOR THIS CHUTNEY HAS A PRETTY GREEN COLOR AND BRIGHTENS ANY TABLE. CHARMAINE.*

1 cup (4 oz) firmly packed mint leaves
6 scallions (spring onions), including green leaves
2 fresh green chilies, roughly chopped
$1/2$ teaspoon chopped garlic, optional
1 teaspoon salt
2 teaspoons sugar
1 teaspoon garam masala (see page 12)
$1/3$ cup lemon juice
2 tablespoons water

In the absence of the grinding stones used in India for reducing grains to flour, and others which make 'wet' masalas and fresh chutneys, a powerful electric blender is the Western cook's best friend when preparing Indian food.

Put mint into blender together with onions cut into short lengths and all other ingredients. Blend on high speed to a smooth purée. If blender is not available finely chop mint, onions, and chilies and pound a little at a time in mortar and pestle. Then mix in remaining ingredients.

Pack the chutney into a small dish, smooth the surface, cover and chill. Serve as an accompaniment with rice and curries, chapatis, thosai, and other savory snacks.

*INDONESIA*

# BASIC SAMBAL SEASONING
~

*A QUICK METHOD TO PRESENT THE MYRIAD DISHES THAT COMPRISE AN INDONESIAN MEAL. IF YOU LIKE HOT FOOD YOU WILL FIND IT USEFUL TO MAKE UP A QUANTITY OF THIS BASE, WHICH YOU CAN KEEP BOTTLED IN THE REFRIGERATOR READY TO ADD TO INGREDIENTS SUCH AS BOILED OR FRIED POTATOES, BREADFRUIT, YAMS OR OTHER STARCHY VEGETABLES; HARD-BOILED EGGS; BEAN CURD; FRESH OR DRIED FISH, FRIED; FRIED SHRIMP AND OTHER SHELL FISH; CRISP-FRIED STRIPS OF MEAT OR LIVER. THERE IS NO END TO THE VARIATIONS ON THIS THEME. CHARMAINE.*

15–20 large dried chilies
3 large onions, roughly chopped
8 cloves garlic
2 teaspoons dried shrimp paste
$1/2$ cup peanut oil, or more as required
1 cup (12 fl oz, 250 ml) tamarind liquid
3 teaspoons salt
2 tablespoons palm sugar or substitute

Soak chilies in hot water for 20 minutes. In container of electric blender grind the soaked chilies, onions, garlic, and shrimp paste, with enough oil to help the blades draw down the solid ingredients: it may be necessary to use more than half the oil, depending on the size and shape of the blender. When blended to a smooth paste, heat remaining oil in a wok or frying pan and when hot put in the blended ingredients. Fry over medium heat, stirring constantly, until mixture is cooked and dark in color and oil separates and shows around edges. Wash out blender container with the tamarind liquid, add to pan with salt and sugar and simmer for a few minutes longer, stirring. Cool completely and bottle. Store in refrigerator. (If mixture has been cooked in a wok, turn it into a glass or earthenware bowl to cool.)

To use: Heat the required amount (in the proportions of approximately 1 tablespoon to 250 g or 8 oz of the main ingredient) and stir-fry the already-cooked main ingredient in it briefly. If a gravy is required, add $1/2$–1 cup (4–8 fl oz) thick coconut cream and heat to simmering point, stirring constantly.

*INDIA*

# SPICED SPINACH
∾

SERVES: 4

1 lb (500 g) spinach
2 teaspoons toasted cumin seeds, crushed
1 clove garlic crushed with ¹/₂ teaspoon salt
1 teaspoon finely chopped fresh ginger
1 green chili, finely chopped
salt to taste
¹/₂ teaspoon garam masala
1 cup (12 fl oz, 250 ml) natural yogurt

Wash spinach, place in a saucepan with ¹/₂ cup water, cover and cook for 10 minutes. Drain and place spinach in container of electric blender and purée at high speed. Remove, drain and set aside. Toast cumin seeds in a dry pan till brown and fragrant, set aside.

Add garlic, ginger, chili, salt, and garam masala to yogurt and mix well. Place spinach on serving dish, spread over with yogurt mixture and sprinkle with crushed cumin. Serve with boiled rice and curry.

*SRI LANKA*

# CUCUMBER SAMBOL
∾

1 large or 2 small green cucumbers
2 teaspoons salt
¹/₂ cup (4 fl oz) thick coconut cream
1 fresh red chili, seeded and sliced
1 fresh green chili, seeded and sliced
1 small onion, cut in paper-thin slices
2 tablespoons lemon juice

Peel cucumber and slice very thinly. Put in a bowl, sprinkle with salt, and let stand for at least 30 minutes. Press out all liquid and if too salty, rinse with cold water. Drain well.

Mix with remaining ingredients and serve as an accompaniment to a curry meal.

*INDONESIA*

# FRIED CHILI SAMBAL
∾

*COOLED, THEN STORED IN AN AIRTIGHT BOTTLE, THIS SAMBAL WILL KEEP FOR WEEKS IN THE REFRIGERATOR. WHEN SERVING, USE A TEASPOON FOR PORTIONS AND WARN GUESTS IT SHOULD BE EATEN IN TINY QUANTITIES WITH RICE, NOT BY ITSELF: THIS TORRID SAMBAL IS AN ACQUIRED TASTE. HOWEVER, IT IS ENJOYED ON CRISP CRACKERS, IN SANDWICHES, ON STEAKS — IN FACT THERE IS NO LIMIT TO THE WAYS A SAMBAL ADDICT WLLL USE IT. CHARMAINE.*

YIELD: ABOUT 1 CUP

6 large fresh red chilies, roughly chopped
1 large onion
6 cloves garlic
3 tablespoons peanut oil
8 candle nuts or 5 Brazil nuts, finely grated
¹/₂ teaspoon laos powder
1 tablespoon dried shrimp paste
1 teaspoon salt
5 tablespoons tamarind liquid
2 tablespoons palm sugar or substitute

Put chilies, onion, and garlic in container of electric blender and blend to a pulp. If blender is small, blend in small portions. It might be necessary to stop and start the motor several times to draw the onions and chilies down on to the blades. When everything has been blended smoothly, heat the oil in a small frying pan or a saucepan and fry the blended mixture over low heat, stirring, for 5 minutes or until well cooked but not brown. Add candle nuts, laos, dried shrimp paste, and salt. Crush the shrimp paste against the side of the pan and fry, stirring, until mixture is well blended.

Add tamarind liquid and sugar, stir and simmer until well fried and reddish-brown in color and the oil separates from the mixture. Cool. This sambal is not served hot from the fire.

*Note:* If electric blender is not available, seed the chilies and chop very finely. Peel and chop onion finely, crush garlic with salt, then proceed as above.

*INDIA*

# ONION & TOMATO SAMBAL

∾

*THE SWEET-SOUR FLAVORS OF TAMARIND AND SUGAR RAISE THIS ABOVE THE ORDINARY RUN-OF-THE-MILL CLASS OF SAMBALS. CHARMAINE.*

SERVES: 6

2 medium onions

salt

1 tablespoon tamarind pulp or 1 teaspoon instant tamarind

$^1/_4$ cup (2 fl oz, 60 ml) hot water

2 tablespoons brown sugar or jaggery (palm sugar)

2 firm ripe tomatoes

1 tablespoon finely shredded fresh ginger

2 or 3 fresh red or green chilies, seeded and sliced

2 tablespoons chopped cilantro (fresh coriander leaves)

Peel the onions, cut them in halves lengthwise and then cut across into fine slices. Sprinkle generously with salt and leave for an hour. Press out all the liquid and rinse once in cold water. Drain well.

Soak tamarind pulp in hot water for a few minutes, then squeeze to dissolve pulp and strain, discarding the seeds. If using instant tamarind, dissolve in the hot water. Dissolve brown sugar in the tamarind liquid.

Scald tomatoes, peel, and dice. Combine all the ingredients, add salt to taste, chill, and serve. Salads of this type are served as accompaniments to rice and curries.

*SRI LANKA*

# RED COCONUT SAMBOL

∾

*THIS IS ONE OF REUBEN'S FAVOURITE SAMBOLS. HE PREFERS IT WITH $^1/_2$ TEASPOON CRUSHED GARLIC ADDED TO THE RECIPE, BUT WHETHER YOU FOLLOW HIS IDEA OR NOT DEPENDS ON YOUR LEVEL OF GARLIC TOLERANCE AND THAT OF YOUR CLOSE ASSOCIATES! CHARMAINE.*

SERVES: 6–8

1 cup (3 oz) unsweetened desiccated coconut

1 teaspoon salt

1–2 teaspoons chili powder, to taste

2 teaspoons paprika (for color)

2 teaspoons maldive fish or prawn powder, optional

3 tablespoons lemon juice

1 small onion, finely chopped

2 fresh red or green chilies, seeded and chopped

Combine all the ingredients in a bowl and mix with your hands, so that the coconut is moistened by the onion and lemon juice. If necessary sprinkle a couple of tablespoons of hot water over so that the coconut is thoroughly moistened.

See picture opposite page 98.

*INDIA*

# BANANA RAITA

∾

SERVES: 6

3 large ripe bananas

lemon juice

1 cup (8 fl oz, 250 ml) natural yogurt

3 tablespoons freshly grated or unsweetened desiccated coconut

$^1/_2$ teaspoon salt

2 teaspoons sugar

$^1/_2$ teaspoon ground toasted cumin seeds

Slice the bananas and sprinkle with lemon juice. Combine the yogurt with the other ingredients. If unsweetened desiccated coconut is used, moisten it first by sprinkling with about 2 tablespoons water and tossing it with the fingers until it is no longer dry. Chill and serve.

See picture opposite page 98.

*BURMA*

# POUNDED SHRIMP PASTE

~

*I MUST WARN READERS THAT IT TAKES SOMEONE BORN OR BROUGHT UP IN BURMA TO FULLY APPRECIATE THIS PUNGENT PASTE. CHARMAINE.*

2 tablespoons shrimp (prawn) powder
2 tablespoons dried shrimp paste
2 medium onions
4 cloves garlic
2 teaspoons chili powder, optional
1 teaspoon salt
juice of half a lemon

Press dried shrimp paste into a flat cake, wrap in foil and put under a hot broiler grill for 15 minutes, turning to cook both sides. Wrap onions and garlic in foil and put under broiler with the dried shrimp paste. Pound together these ingredients in a mortar and pestle. Mix in remaining ingredients.

Alternatively, the crumbled dried shrimp paste, peeled onions, and garlic can be blended in an electric blender with lemon juice and combined with other ingredients.

*SRI LANKA*

# GROUND ONION & CHILI SAMBOL

~

*THIS SIMPLE SAMBOL IS AS BASIC TO THE FOOD OF SRI LANKA AS SALT AND PEPPER ARE TO WESTERN FOOD. CHARMAINE.*

10 dried chilies
1 tablespoon pounded maldive fish or dried shrimp (prawns)
1 small onion, chopped
lemon juice and salt to taste

Remove stalks from chilies. If a less hot result is preferred, shake out the seeds. Pound all the ingredients together in a mortar and pestle. In Sri Lanka this would be either pounded or ground on the grinding stone. Serve with rice.

*MALAYSIA*

# BEEF SAMBAL

~

*WHEN WE WERE SERVED THIS IN KUALA LUMPUR, FRESH LAOS WAS USED, AND THE GARLIC STEPPED UP. VERY INTERESTING INDEED. REUBEN.*

SERVES: 4

8 oz (250 g) scotch filet, sliced thin
2 tablespoons peanut oil
5 candlenuts or 4 Brazil kernels, chopped
1 teaspoon dried shrimp paste
2 medium onions, roughly chopped
5 dried red chilies
$^1/_2$ teaspoon ground turmeric
1 teaspoon ground laos
1 teaspoon chopped garlic
1 teaspoon tamarind paste
1 teaspoon salt
2 teaspoons sugar

Slice beef into thin shreds. Blend all ingredients except oil to a fine paste in an electric blender, adding a little hot water to facilitate blending.

Heat oil in saucepan or wok. Add mixture to hot oil and stir-fry till mixture smells cooked and oil surfaces. Add sliced beef and stir till well coated with mixture. Cover and simmer till gravy thickens (about 5 minutes). Serve with boiled rice and curry.

*THAILAND*

# FRESH LEMON GRASS SALAD

~

4 stems lemon grass
5 fresh red chilies, chopped
1-2 tablespoons fish sauce (see Glossary)

Use only the pale, tender base of the lemon grass. Wash well and chop finely. Place in a bowl, add chilies and fish sauce. Mix well and serve with curry and boiled rice.

*MALAYSIA*

# OMELET SAMBAL

∾

SERVES: 4-6

4 eggs, slightly beaten
3 tablespoons peanut oil
1 large onion, finely sliced
2 red chilies
1 teaspoon dried shrimp paste
1 teaspoon garlic chopped
$^1/_2$ teaspoon ground black pepper
salt to taste

Heat oil in a wok or saucepan. Fry onion till soft and golden. Blend chilies, dried shrimp paste, garlic, pepper, and salt to a paste in an electric blender, adding a little water to facilitate blending. Add spice mixture to onions and stir-fry till mixture smells fragrant, and oil comes to the surface. Stir in beaten eggs and cook into one large omelet. Divide into 4 to 6 segments and serve with rice and curry.

*INDONESIA*

# PIQUANT FRIED SHRIMP SAMBAL

∾

SERVES: 6

1 lb (500 g) shelled raw shrimp (prawns)
2 tablespoons peanut oil
1 onion, finely chopped
$1^1/_2$ teaspoons finely chopped garlic
$^1/_2$ teaspoon finely grated fresh ginger
2 teaspoons sambal ulek (see Glossary)
or 4 fresh red chilies
$^1/_2$ teaspoon laos powder
2 strips thinly peeled lemon rind, chopped
1/3 cup tamarind liquid (see Glossary)
1 teaspoon salt
1 teaspoon palm sugar (jaggery) or substitute

If shrimp are large, chop shrimp into pieces the size of a peanut. Small shrimp may be used whole. Heat oil in a frying pan and fry onion, garlic, and ginger until onion is soft and starts to turn golden. Add sambal ulek, laos powder, and lemon rind, then add chopped shrimp and fry, stirring constantly, until shrimp turn pink.

Add tamarind liquid and simmer on low heat until gravy is thick and oil starts to separate. Stir in salt and sugar. Taste and correct seasoning if necessary. Serve as a side dish with rice and curries.

*MALAYSIA*

# SAMBAL UDANG

∾

SERVES: 6

$1^1/_2$ lb (750 g) medium-sized shrimp,
shelled and deveined
2 tablespoons peanut oil
6 dried red chilies
1 medium onion, roughly chopped
6 candlenuts, or 4 Brazil kernels, chopped
1 teaspoon dried shrimp paste
2 teaspoons chopped garlic
1 teaspoon chopped fresh ginger
2 teaspoons tamarind paste
1 teaspoon salt
2 teaspoons sugar

Place chilies, onion, kernels, dried shrimp paste, garlic, ginger, and tamarind paste in container of electric blender. Add a little water to assist movement of the blades, and blend to a smooth paste.

Heat wok or saucepan, add oil and when hot add blended mixture. Stir-fry for a few minutes till mixture smells cooked and oil comes to the surface. Add shrimp and stir-fry till well coated with the mixture then add salt and sugar. Continue to stir-fry till shrimp are cooked and gravy thickens. Serve with rice and curry.

*THAILAND*

# BRAISED BITTER MELON SALAD
∾

2 x 3 in (7.5 cm) tender bitter melon
1 tablespoon peanut oil
2 teaspoons grated garlic
4 fresh red chilies, chopped
1 tablespoon shrimp (prawn) powder
1–2 tablespoons fish sauce (see Glossary)
$^1/_2$ teaspoon ground black pepper

Cut bitter melon lengthwise in half. Slice thinly across and set aside. Heat wok, add oil and when hot, stir-fry the bitter melon for 1 minute, then stir in the garlic and red chilies for another minute. Add the rest of the ingredients. Stir and cover for 1 more minute, then remove to a dish. Serve with curry and boiled rice.

*BURMA*

# SHRIMP PASTE SAUTE
∾

*I FIRST TRIED THIS IN MANDALAY AND HAVE BEEN HOOKED ON IT EVER SINCE. REUBEN.*

$^1/_2$ cup (4 fl oz, 125 ml) vegetable oil
1 onion, chopped
3 teaspoons finely chopped garlic
$^1/_4$ teaspoon turmeric
1 tablespoon dried shrimp paste
3–4 tomatoes, quartered
1 cup (3 oz, 90 g)) dried shrimp (prawn) powder
2 green chilies, sliced
1 tablespoon tamarind liquid (see Glossary)
$^1/_2$ teaspoon salt or to taste

Heat oil until very hot, reduce heat to medium and fry onion, garlic, and turmeric till dark golden and nearly catching to pan. Add dried shrimp paste, tomatoes, shrimp powder, green chilies, and tamarind liquid. Stir and cook until all the liquid has evaporated and oil separates from the mass. Add salt to taste.

*INDIA*

# BOMBAY DUCK
∾

*A PUNGENT DRIED FISH WHICH IS SERVED AS AN ACCOMPANIMENT TO RICE AND CURRY MEALS. SOLD IN PACKETS, THEY SHOULD BE CUT INTO PIECES ABOUT 2 IN (5 CM) IN LENGTH AND DEEP FRIED IN HOT OIL UNTIL LIGHT GOLDEN BROWN. DRAIN AND SERVE AS A CRISP NIBBLE BETWEEN MOUTHFULS OF RICE.*

An alternative method is to fry finely sliced onions in the same oil after the Bombay ducks are fried, and if liked, some broken dried chilies may be fried along with the onions. Fry slowly, stirring, until onions are golden brown. Add a little salt and sugar, stir well, combine with the fried Bombay duck and serve as a sambal.

*SRI LANKA*

# SHRIMP BLACHAN
∾

*IN COLOMBO, FRESH COCONUT IS USED AND THE INGREDIENTS GROUND ON A STONE. IT IS ONE OF THE "SPECIAL OCCASION" ACCOMPANIMENTS. CHARMAINE.*

1 cup (4 oz, 125 g) dried shrimp (prawn) powder
$^1/_2$ cup ($1^1/_2$ oz, 45 g) unsweetened desiccated coconut
2 teaspoons chili powder or to taste
2 medium onions, chopped
5 cloves garlic, sliced
1 tablespoon finely chopped fresh ginger
$^2/_3$ cup lemon juice
1 teaspoon salt, or to taste

Put shrimp powder in a dry frying pan and heat for a few minutes, stirring. Turn onto a large plate. Put unsweetened desiccated coconut in the same pan and heat, stirring, until a rich brown color. Turn onto a plate to cool.

Put other ingredients except shrimp powder into blender container, cover and blend until smooth. Add shrimp powder and unsweetened desiccated coconut, cover and blend again, adding a little water if necessary to bind ingredients. Scrape down sides of container occasionally with a spatula. Turn onto a plate and shape into a round, flat cake. Serve with rice and curries.

*INDIA*

# BEETROOT RAITA
~

*CHARMAINE'S RECIPE BELOW IS A CLASSIC. SPRINKLE IT WITH*
*A TEASPOON OF LIGHTLY TOASTED GROUND CUMIN TO SEE*
*WHAT HAPPENS. REUBEN.*

SERVES: 4

1 cup (5 oz, 155 g) canned beetroot
1 cup (8 fl oz, 250 ml) natural yogurt
salt to taste

Chop the beetroot roughly and mix into the yogurt, adding a little of the juice from the can to give color and flavor. Taste and add more salt if desired. Chill and serve cold as a cooling accompaniment to a curry meal.

See picture opposite page 98.

*BURMA*

# DRY BALACHAUNG
~

*BRINGS BACK MEMORIES OF BURMA. IN AN ORTHODOX JEWISH*
*HOME WE SUBSTITUTED MERGUI SALT FISH FOR THE SHRIMP.*
*EVEN GREAT AS A SANDWICH FILLING. REUBEN.*

20 cloves garlic 4 medium onions, finely sliced
2 cups (16 fl oz, 500 ml) peanut oil
1 x 8 oz (250 g) packet of shrimp (prawn) powder
teaspoons chili powder, optional
2 teaspoons salt
1 teaspoon dried shrimp paste
$^1/_2$ cup (4 fl oz, 125 ml) vinegar

Peel garlic, cut into thin slices. Cut onions into thin slices. Heat oil and fry onion and garlic separately on low heat until golden. Lift out immediately and set aside.

Pour off all but 1 cup (8 fl oz, 250 ml) oil and in this, fry shrimp powder for 5 minutes. Add chili powder, salt, and shrimp paste mixed with vinegar, stir well and fry until crisp. Allow to cool completely. Mix in fried onion and garlic, stirring to distribute evenly. Store in an airtight jar. Serve with rice or noodles, and Burmese curries.

See pictures opposite page 35 and 98.

*INDIA*

# TOMATO &
# SCALLION SAMBAL
~

*TRY THIS SPRINKLED OVER WITH $^1/_2$ TEASPOON GARAM MASALA.*
*REUBEN.*
*I DON'T AGREE. I LIKE IT JUST THE WAY IT IS. CHARMAINE.*

SERVES: 4

2 large firm red tomatoes
$^1/_2$ cup (2 oz, 60 g) finely chopped scallions
(spring onions), green leaves and all
$^1/_2$ teaspoon chili powder
$^1/_2$ teaspoons salt or to taste
2–3 tablespoons lemon juice

Cut the tomatoes in small dice and sprinkle with all the other ingredients, tossing gently until well mixed. Cover and chill until required and serve as an accompaniment to rice and curry.

See picture opposite page 98.

*INDIA*

# CILANTRO &
# COCONUT
# CHUTNEY
~

*ANYTHING WITH CILANTRO (FRESH CORIANDER LEAVES) AND*
*GARLIC IN IT PLEASES REUBEN IMMENSELY.. CHARMAINE.*

SERVES: 6

1 cup (8 oz, 250 g) cilantro (fresh coriander leaves)
2 tablespoons unsweetened desiccated coconut
3 tablespoons water
1 teaspoon chopped garlic
1 green chili, seeded
1 teaspoon garam masala (see page 12)
1 teaspoon salt
2 tablespoons lemon juice

Put the well-washed cilantro into container of electric blender with all other ingredients and blend on high speed until smooth. If necessary, add a little water to facilitate blending, but do not make the mixture too wet.

See picture opposite page 98.

*INDIA*

# COCONUT CHUTNEY
∾

*ASAFOETIDA! THAT'S REUBEN'S TOUCH. TRY IT AS DIRECTED FOR A NEW DIMENSION IN TASTE. CHARMAINE.*

SERVES: 6–8

$^1/_2$ a coconut, freshly grated or 1 cup (3 oz, 90 g)
unsweetened/desiccated coconut
1 lemon or lime
2 or 3 fresh green chilies
$^1/_2$ cup (3/4 oz, 21 g) chopped fresh mint
1 teaspoon salt
2 teaspoons ghee or oil
$^1/_8$ teaspoon ground asafoetida (see Glossary), optional
1 teaspoon black mustard seeds
1 teaspoon black cumin seeds
10 curry leaves
$^1/_2$ teaspoon urad dhal

If using desiccated coconut, sprinkle with about $^1/_4$ cup (2 fl oz, 60 ml) water and toss to moisten evenly. Peel the lemon or lime so that no white pith remains. Cut in pieces and remove the seeds. Put lemon into container of electric blender with the seeded and roughly chopped chilies and mint and blend until smooth. Add the coconut and continue blending to a smooth paste, scraping down sides of blender and adding a little more liquid if necessary. Add the salt and mix.

Heat ghee or oil in a small pan and fry the remaining ingredients, stirring frequently, until mustard seeds pop and dhal is golden. Mix with the coconut, pat into a flat cake and serve as an accompaniment to a curry meal.

See picture opposite page 82.

# PAPPADAMS
∾

ALLOW 2 PER PERSON

pappadams
peanut oil for deep frying

These spicy lentil wafers are sold dried in packets. Heat the oil and test with a small piece of pappadam: if the oil is not hot enough the piece will sink to the bottom and stay there. The oil should be hot enough for the pappadam to double its size within the first two or three seconds.

Deep fry one pappadam at a time for three or four seconds in the oil. They will swell and turn pale golden. Drain well on absorbent paper. Pappadams are best fried just before serving, but they may be cooled and stored in an airtight container if prepared a few hours beforehand.

See picture opposite page 98.

*SRI LANKA*

# FRIED EGGPLANT SAMBOL
∾

2 eggplants (aubergines)
2 teaspoons salt
2 teaspoons ground turmeric
oil for frying
3 fresh red or green chilies
2 small onions
lemon juice
3 tablespoons thick coconut cream

Slice eggplants thinly, rub with salt and turmeric, put in a bowl and leave at least 1 hour. Drain off liquid and dry eggplant on paper towels.

Fry in hot oil and drain on absorbent paper. Mix with seeded and chopped chilies, finely sliced onion, lemon juice to taste, and thick coconut cream.

SRI LANKA

# ROASTED COCONUT SAMBOL

∾

*IN SRI LANKA, THIS IS A VERY POPULAR ACCOMPANIMENT TO A MEAL OF RICE AND CURRIES. THE FRESH COCONUT IS HALVED, ROASTED IN THE ASHES OF A FIRE UNTIL DARK BROWN, THEN GROUND ON A STONE. THIS IS THE EASY METHOD THAT I HAD TO LEARN WHEN DEPRIVED OF A CONSTANT SUPPLY OF FRESH COCONUTS AND HOUSEHOLD HELP TO GRIND THEM! CHARMAINE.*

1 cup (3 oz, 90 g) unsweetened desiccated coconut
2 medium onions, finely chopped
1 teaspoon salt
2 teaspoons maldive fish or dried shrimp (prawn) powder
4 tablespoons lemon juice or to taste

In a heavy based frying pan heat the coconut, stirring constantly so it will brown evenly. It should be a deep brown, not merely golden, so that it gives this sambol its distinctive taste. Remove from pan immediately and spread on a plate to cool. Combine all ingredients in electric blender, cover and blend until a smooth paste is formed. If liquid is insufficient it may be necessary to add a little more lemon juice or finely grated onion. Shape the paste into a flat cake on a small plate. Mark the top in a criss-cross pattern with the back of a knife.

MALAYSIA

# MALAY VEGETABLE PICKLES

∾

1 cup (2$^1$/$_2$ oz, 75 g) carrot sticks
1 cup (2$^1$/$_2$ oz, 75 g) green (string) beans
10 fresh red and green chilies
1 green cucumber
$^1$/$_2$ a small cauliflower
2 tablespoons peanut oil
1 teaspoon finely chopped garlic
2 teaspoons finely grated fresh ginger
3 candlenuts or Brazil kernels, grated
1 teaspoon ground turmeric
$^1$/$_2$ cup (4 fl oz, 125 ml) white vinegar
$^1$/$_2$ cup (4 fl oz, 125 ml) water
2 teaspoons sugar
1 teaspoon salt

Cut carrots into julienne strips. Cut beans into pieces of the same length, then slice each piece in two lengthwise. If beans are very young and slender it will not be necessary to slice them. Leave the chilies whole, but remove stems. Peel cucumber and cut in half lengthwise, remove seeds and slice into pieces the same size as the carrots and beans. Cut cauliflowers into sprigs leaving a bit of stem on each piece.

Heat oil in a saucepan and fry garlic and ginger on low heat for 1 minute, stirring. Add grated nuts and turmeric and stir for a few seconds longer. Add vinegar, water, sugar, and salt and bring to a boil. Add carrots, beans, chilies, and cauliflower sprigs, return to a boil and boil for 3 minutes. Add cucumber and boil for 1 minute longer.

Remove immediately to an earthenware or glass bowl and allow to cool. Use at once or bottle and store in refrigerator for a week or two.

# Glossary

## AJOWAN (AJWAIN)

Bot: *Carum ajowan*
Fam: *Umbelliferae*
Hindi: *ajwain*

Of the same family as parsley and cumin, the seeds look like parsley or celery seeds, but have the flavor of thyme. It is used in Indian cooking, particularly in lentil dishes that provide the protein in vegetarian diets, both as a flavoring and as a carminative. It is one of the seeds used to flavor the crisp-fried snacks made from lentil flour. Ajwain water is used as a medicine in stomach ailments.

## AMCHUR

Dried green mango, usually available in powder form. Used as an acid flavoring ingredient in Indian cooking.

## AROMATIC GINGER

see Galangal, lesser

## ASAFOETIDA

Bot: Ferula *asafoetida*
Fam: *Umbelliferae*
Hindi: *hing*
Tamil: *perunkaya*
Burmese: *sheingho*

Used in minute quantities in Indian cooking, its main purpose is to prevent flatulence. It is obtained from the resinous gum of a plant growing in Afghanistan and Iran. The stalks are cut close to the root and the milky fluid that flows out is dried into the resin sold as asafoetida. Although it has quite an unpleasant smell by itself a tiny piece the size of a pea attached to the inside of the lid of a cooking pot adds a certain flavor that is much prized, apart from its medicinal properties.

## ATTA

Fine wholewheat (wholemeal) flour used in making Indian flat breads. Substitute fine wholewheat flour sold in health food stores. Atta flour can be bought from stores specialising in Asian foods.

## BAMBOO SHOOT

Malay: *rebong*
Indonesian: *rebung*

Sold in cans, either water-packed or braised. Unless otherwise stated, the recipes in this book use the water-packed variety. After opening can, store in a bowl of fresh water in the refrigerator, changing water daily, for up to 10 days. Winter bamboo shoots are much smaller and more tender, and are called for in certain recipes; however, if they are not available, use the larger variety.

## BASIL (SWEET BASIL)

Bot: Ocimum *basilicum*
Fam: *Labiatae*
Hindi: *babuitulsi*
Thai: *horapa*

*Accompaniments to a curry meal: Tomato and Scallion Sambal, Beetroot Raita, Cilantro and Coconut Chutney, Dry Balachaung (all on page 95), Red Coconut Sambol (page 91), grilled Pappadams (page 96), and Banana Raita (page 91).*

*Indian breads: from the top, cooked chapatis (page 26), puris (page 27) and parathas (page 27) in the making.*

Malay: *selaseb, kemangi*
Indonesian: *kemangi*

Used in Indonesian cooking, the leaves add distinctive flavor to those dishes requiring it.

## BAY

Bot: *Laurus nobilis*
Fam: *Lauraceae*

Almost universally used in European cooking. There is a rather similar leaf, known as tejpattar, used in Indian cooking.

## BEAN SPROUTS

Green mung beans are normally used for bean sprouts. They are sold fresh in most Chinese stores and in certain supermarkets and health food stores. The canned variety is not recommended. Substitute thinly sliced celery for a similar texture but different flavor. Fresh bean sprouts can be stored in a refrigerator for a week in a plastic bag; alternatively, cover with water and change water daily.

## BESAN
## (CHICKPEA FLOUR)

Available in most stores selling Asian foods. Pea flour from health food stores can be substituted, but if it is coarse pass it through a fine sieve before using. Alternatively, roast yellow split peas in a heavy pan, stirring constantly and taking care not to burn them. Cool, then blend at high speed in an electric blender or pound with a mortar and pestle. Sift, then store the fine flour in an airtight container. Besan has a distinctive taste, and ordinary wheat flour cannot be substituted.

## BITTER MELON
## (BALSAM PEAR)

Belonging to the squash family, this vegetable can best be described as looking like a cucumber with lumps. Its bitterness is due to the high quinine content. During the season it may be obtained fresh from Chinese produce stores, or canned, from Asian specialty stores. As a fresh vegetable, its refrigerator life is 10 to 12 days. It may be used in stir-fries with meats or alone as a vegetable dish.

## BLACHAN

The commercial spelling of blacan. See dried shrimp paste.

## BOMBAY DUCK

Not a bird, despite its name, this is a variety of fish that is salted and dried. It is sold in packets and should be cut into pieces no more than 1 inch (2.5 cm) long. Deep fried or broiled (grilled), it is served as an accompaniment to a meal of rice and curry, and should be nibbled in little pieces.

## CANDLENUT

Bot: *Aleurites moluccana*
Fam: *Euphorbiaceae*
Malay: *buah keras*
Indonesian: *kemiri*

A hard oily nut used to flavor and thicken Indonesian and Malaysian curries. The name arises because the nuts, when threaded on the midrib of a palm leaf, are used as a primitive candle. Use Brazil kernels as a substitute, though their flavor is sweeter than that of the candlenut.

## CARDAMOM

Bot: *Elettaria cardamomum*
Fam: *Zingiberaceae*
Hindi: *illaichi*
Sinhalese: *enasal*
Burmese: *phalazee*
Thai: *kravan*
Malay: *buah pelaga*
Indonesian: *kapulaga*

Next to saffron, the world's most expensive spice. Cardamoms grow mainly in India and

Ceylon, and are the seed pods of a member of the ginger family. The dried seed pods are either pale green or brown, according to variety. Sometimes they are bleached white. They are added, either whole or bruised, to pilaus and other rice dishes, spiced curries and other preparations or sweets. When ground cardamom is called for, the seed pods are opened and discarded and only the small black or brown seeds are ground. For full flavor, it is best to grind them just before using. There is one brand of "ground decorticated cardamom" that seems to preserve extremely well the essential oils and fragrances of this exotic spice, but if you cannot buy a really good ground cardamom, crush the seeds in a mortar as required.

## CASHEW NUT (CASHEWS)

Hindi: *kaju*
Malay: *gaju*
Sinhalese: *cadju*

A sweet, kidney-shaped nut. In countries where the cashew tree is not grown, it is not possible to get the milky sweet fresh cashews. However, it is possible to buy raw cashews (as distinct from the roasted and salted cashews sold as snacks); nut shops, health food stores and stores specialising in Asian ingredients stock the raw cashews.

## CELLOPHANE NOODLES OR BEAN THREAD VERMICELLI

Thai: *woon sen*
Malay: *sohoon, tunghoon*
Indonesian: *sotanghoon*

Fine, transparent noodles made from the starch of green mung beans. May be soaked in hot water before use, or may require boiling according to the texture required. They are also deep fried straight from the packet, generally when used as a garnish or to provide a background for other foods.

## CHILI POWDER

Asian chili powder is made from ground chilies. It is much hotter than the Mexican style chili powder, which is mostly ground cumin.

## CHILI SAUCE

There are two different types of chili sauce. The Chinese style is made from chilies, salt, and vinegar, and has a hot flavor. The Malaysian, Singaporean, or Sri Lankan chili sauce is a mixture of hot, sweet, and salty flavors generously laced with ginger and garlic and cooked with vinegar. It is easy to buy both types.

## CHILIES, BIRD'S EYE OR BIRD PEPPERS

Very small, very hot chilies. Used mainly in pickles, though in some cases added to food when a very hot flavor is required (as in Thai food). Treat with extreme caution.

## CHILIES, BELL PEPPERS (CAPSICUMS) OR PEPPERS

Bot: *Capsicum frutescens or capsicum annuum*
Fam: *Solanaceae*
Sinhalese: *malu miris*

A much milder though still flavorful variety of chili with a long pod large enough to stuff with spiced meat or fish mixtures.

## CHILIES, GREEN

Bot: *Capsicum* spp.
Hindi: *subz mirich*
Sinhalese: *amu miris*
Thai: *nil thee sein*
Malay: *chili, cabai hijau*
Indonesian: *lombok hijau*

Used like fresh red chilies. Sometimes ground into sambals. The seeds, which are the hottest parts, are usually (though not always) removed.

# CHILIES, RED

Bot: *Capsicum* spp.
Hindi: *lal mirich*
Sinhalese: *rathu miris*
Burmese: *nil-thee*
Thai: *prik chee pha*
Tamil: *kochikai*
Malay: *cabai, chili*
Indonesian: *lombok*

Used fresh for flavoring, either whole or finely chopped; or sliced for garnishes.

# CINNAMON

Bot: *Cinnamomum zeylanicum*
Fam: *Lauraceae*
Hindi: *darchini*
Sinhalese: *kurundu*
Thai: *op chery*
Burmese: *thit-ja-boh-gauk*
Malay: *kayu manis*
Indonesian: *kayu manis*

True cinnamon is native to Sri Lanka. Buy cinnamon sticks or quills rather than the ground spice, which loses its flavor when stored too long. It is used in both sweet and savory dishes.

Cassia, which is grown in India, Indonesia, and Burma, is similar. It is much stronger in flavor, and is cheaper, but it lacks the delicacy of cinnamon. The leaves and buds of the cassia tree have a flavor similar to the bark and are also used for flavoring food. For sweet dishes especially it is best to use true cinnamon. Look for the thin pale bark, sun-dried to form quills that are packed one inside the other. Cassia bark is much thicker because the corky layer is left on.

# CLOVES

Bot: *Eugenia aromatica*
Fam: *Myrtaceae*
Hindi: *laung*
Sinhalese: *karabu*
Burmese: *ley-nyin-bwint*
Malay: *bunga cingkeh*
Indonesian: *cenkeh*

Cloves are the dried flower buds of an evergreen tropical tree native to Southeast Asia. They were used in China more than 2000 years ago, and were also used by the Romans. Oil of cloves contains phenol, a powerful antiseptic that discourages putrefaction, and the clove is hence one of the spices that helps preserve food.

# COCONUT CREAM

This is the creamy liquid that is extracted from the grated flesh of fresh coconuts or from the unsweetened desiccated (shredded) coconut. It is also available in cans. When coconut cream is called for, do try to use it, for the coconut flavor cannot be duplicated by using any other kind of cream or milk. See page 8.

# CORIANDER

Bot: *Coriandrum sativum*
Fam: *Umbelliferae*
Hindi: *dhania (seed), dhania pattar, dhania sabz (leaves)*
Sinhalese: *kottamalli (seed), kottamalli kolle (leaves)*
Burmese: *nannamzee (seed), nannambin (leaves)*
Thai: *pak chee*
Malay: *ketumbar (seeds), daun ketumbar (leaves)*

All parts of the coriander plant are used in Asian cooking. The dried seed is the main ingredient in curry powder, and although not hot it has a fragrance that makes it an essential part of a curry blend. The fresh coriander leaf is also called Chinese parsley or cilantro. Although it may take some getting used to because of its pungent smell (the name comes from the Greek koris, meaning "bug"), Southeast Asian food is not the same without it. It is indispensable in Burma, Thailand, Vietnam, India, and China where it is also called "fragrant green". If you have difficulty obtaining it, grow fresh coriander yourself in a small patch of garden or even a window box. Scatter the seeds, sprinkle lightly with soil and water every day. They take about 18 days to germinate. Pick them when about 6 in (15 cm) high and do not allow plants to go to seed.

# CUMIN OR CUMMIN

Bot: *Cuminum cyminum*
Fam: *Umbelliferae*
Hindi: *sufaid zeera (white cumin), zeera, jeera*
Sinhalese: *sududuru*
Thai: *yira*
Malay: *jintan puteh*
Indonesian: *jinten*

Cumin is, with coriander, the most essential ingredient in prepared curry powders. It is available as seed, or ground. There is some confusion between cumin and caraway seeds because they are similar in appearance, but the flavors are completely different and one cannot replace the other in recipes.

## CUMIN, BLACK

Bot: *Nigella sativa*
Fam: *Ranunculaceae*
Hindi: *kala zeera, kalonji*

Although the Indian name kala zeera translates as "black cumin" this is not true cumin and the flavor is different. Aromatic and peppery, Nigella is an essential ingredient in panch phora (see page 12).

## CUMIN, SWEET

see Fennel

## CURRY LEAVES

Bot: *Murraya koenigii*
Fam: *Rutaceae*
Hindi: *kitha neem, katnim, karipattar*
Sinhalese: *karapincha*
Tamil: *karuvepila*
Burmese: *pyi-naw-thein*
Malay: *daun kari, karupillay*

Sold dried, they are as important to curries as bay leaves are to stews, but never try to substitute one for the other. The tree is native to Asia, the leaves are small and very shiny, and though they keep their flavor well when dried they are found in such abundance in Asia that they are generally used fresh. The leaves are fried in oil, until crisp,

at the start of preparing a curry; they can also be pulverized in a blender; and the powdered leaves can be used in marinades and omelets. Substitute daun salam.

## CURRY POWDER

Rarely used in countries where curry is eaten daily (the word comes from the Tamil "kari", meaning "sauce"). It is preferable to roast and grind the spices separately.

## DAUN PANDAN

see Pandanus

## DAUN SALAM

An aromatic leaf used in Indonesian cooking, it is larger than the curry leaf used in India and Sri Lanka, but has a similar flavor. Substitute curry leaves.

## DILL

Bot: *Anethum graveolens*
Fam: *Umbelliferae*
Sinhalese: *enduru*

Much used in Russia and European cooking, this herb is also very popular in Sri Lanka where it gives a distinctive flavor to ground (minced) meat mixtures, frikkadels, fish cutlets, and so on. Similar in appearance to fennel, it is much smaller and grows only to $1^1/2$–3 ft (45-90 cm) in height; the leaf is feathery and thread-like.

## DRIED FISH

Hindi: *nethali*
Sinhalese: *haal masso*
Thai: *plasroi*
Malay: *ikan bilis*
Indonesian: *ikan bilis*

These tiny sprats or anchovies should be rinsed and the intestines removed (if this has not already been done) before use. Avoid soaking them, or they will not retain their crispness when fried. Dry on paper towels before frying.

# DRIED SHRIMP PASTE

Burmese: *ngapi*

Thai: *kapi*

Malay: *blacan*

Indonesian: *trasi*

A pungent paste made from shrimp (prawns), and used in many Southeast Asian recipes. It is sold in cans or flat slabs or cakes and will keep indefinitely. If stored in a tightly closed jar it will, like a genie in a bottle, perform its magic when required without obtruding on the kitchen at other times! It does not need refrigeration. Commercially sold as "blachan" or "belacan".

# FENNEL

Bot: *Foeniculum vulgare*

Fam: *Umbelliferae*

Hindi: *sonf*

Sinhalese: *maduru*

Burmese: *samouk-saba*

Malay: *jintan manis*

Indonesian: *adas*

Sometimes known as "sweet cumin" or "large cumin", it is a member of the same botanical family and is used in Sri Lankan curries (but in much smaller quantities than true cumin). It is available in ground or seed form. Substitute an equal amount of aniseed.

# FENUGREEK

Bot: *Trigonella foenum-graecum*

Fam: *Leguminosae (papilionaceae)*

Hindi: *methi*

Sinhalese: *uluhaal*

Malay: *alba*

These small, flat, squarish, brownish-beige seeds are essential in curries, but because they have a slightly bitter flavor they must be used in the stated quantities. They are especially good in fish curries, where the whole seeds are gently fried at the start of cooking; they are also ground and added to curry powders. The green leaves are used in Indian cooking and, when spiced, the bitter taste is quite piquant and acceptable. The plant is easy to grow, and when at the two-leaf stage it makes a tangy addition to salads.

# FISH SAUCE

Burmese: *ngan-pya-ye*

Thai: *nam pla*

A thin, salty, brown sauce used in Southeast Asian cooking to bring out the flavor in other foods. A small variety of fish is packed in wooden barrels with salt, and the liquid that runs off is the "fish sauce". Substitute light soy sauce, adding to each cup one teaspoon of dried shrimp paste, which has been wrapped in foil and broiled (grilled) for 5 minutes on each side and then powdered. Stir well and bottle. Shake bottle before use. There are different grades of fish sauce, the Vietnamese version being darker and having a more pronounced fish flavor than the others.

# GALANGAL, GREATER

Bot: *Alpinia galanga*

Fam: *Zingiberaceae*

Thai: *kha*

Malay: *lengkuas*

Indonesian: *laos*

The greater galangal is more extensively used in Southeast Asian cooking than the lesser, and is more delicate in flavor. It is a rhizome, like ginger, and beneath the thin brown skin the flesh is creamy white; the flesh of lesser galangal has an orange-red hue.

# GALANGAL, LESSER

Bot: *Kaempferia pandurata* or *Alpinia officinarum*

Fam: *Zingiberaceae*

Sinhalese: *ingurupiyali*

Thai: *krachai*

Malay: *zeodary* or *kencur*

Indonesian: *kencur*

Also known as "aromatic ginger", this member of the ginger family cannot be used as a substitute for ginger or vice versa. It is used only in certain dishes, and gives a pronounced aromatic flavor. When available fresh, it is sliced or pounded to a pulp; but outside of Asia it is usually sold dried, and the hard round slices must be pounded with a mortar and pestle or pulverized in a blender before use. In some spice ranges it is sold in powdered form. The plant is native to southern China and has been used for centuries in medicinal herbal mixtures, but it is not used in Chinese cooking.

# GARAM MASALA

A mixture of ground spices used in Indian cooking.

# GARLIC

Bot: *Allium sativum*
Fam: *Liliaceae*
Hindi: *lasan*
Sinhalese: *sudulunu*
Burmese: *chyet-thon-phew*
Malay: *bawang puteh*
Indoneslan: *bawang putih*

Almost universal in application, and vital in Asian cooking (although Kasmiri Brahmins eschew it as inflaming baser passions), garlic is not only a flavoring but is also prized for its health-giving properties. There are many varieties – some with large cloves, some very small; some white, some purplish; some easily peeled, and some with a skin that sticks so closely that it has to be prised off; and some are very strong in flavor, while other types can be quite mild.

# GHEE
# (CLARIFIED BUTTER)

Sold in tins, ghee is pure butter-fat without any of the milk solids. It can be heated to much higher temperatures than butter without burning, and imparts a distinctive flavor when used as a cooking medium.

# GINGER

Bot: *Zingiber officinale*
Fam: *Zingiberaceae*
Hindi: *adrak*
Sinhalese: *inguru*
Burmese: *gin*
Thai: *khing*
Malay: *halia*
Indonesian: *jahe*

A rhizome with a pungent flavor, it is essential in most Asian dishes. Fresh ginger root should be used; powdered ginger cannot be substituted for fresh ginger, for the flavor is quite different. To prepare for use, scrape off the skin with a sharp knife, and either grate or chop finely (according to recipe requirements) before measuring. To preserve fresh ginger for long periods of time, scrape the skin from the rhizome, divide into sections and pack in a well-washed and dried bottle. Pour dry sherry over to completely cover the ginger, cover tightly, and store in the refrigerator.

# GROUND RICE

see Rice, ground

# KEMIRI NUTS

see Candlenut

# KEWRA

see Pandanus odoratissimus

# LAOS

Bot: *Alpinia galanga*

A very delicate spice, sold in powder form, laos comes from the dried root of the "greater galangal". It is so delicate in flavor that it can be omitted from recipes. See galangal.

# LEMON GRASS

Bot: *Cymbopogon citratus*

Fam: *Gramineae*
Hindi: *sera*
Sinhalese: *sera*
Burmese: *zabalin*
Thai: *takrai*
Malay: *serai*
Indonesian: *sereh*

This is an aromatic Asian plant which also grows in Australia, Africa, South America, and Florida (USA). It is a tall grass with sharp-edged leaves that multiply into clumps. The whitish, slightly bulbous base is used to impart a lemony flavor to curries. Cut just one stem with a sharp knife, close to the root, and use about 4–5 in (10–12 cm) of the stalk from the base, discarding the leaves. If using dried lemon grass, about 12 strips dried are equal to one fresh stem; or substitute 2 strips of very thinly peeled lemon rind.

# LIME, SMALL GREEN

Bot: *Citrus microcapa*
Hindi: *nimboo*
Sinhalese: *dehi*
Thai: *ma now*
Malay: *limau nipis, limau kesturi*

The juice of this fruit is used in Asian countries for adding a sour flavor to curries and other dishes. Lemons may be used as a substitute.

# MACE

Bot: *Myristica fragrans*
Fam: *Myristicaceae*
Hindi: *javatri*
Sinhalese: *wasa-vasi*

Mace is part of the nutmeg, a fruit that looks like an apricot and grows on tall tropical trees. When ripe, the fruit splits to reveal the aril, lacy, and bright scarlet, surrounding the shell of the seed; the dried aril is mace and the kernel is nutmeg. Mace has a flavor similar to nutmeg but more delicate, and it is sometimes used in meat or fish curries, especially in Sri Lanka, although its main use in Asia is medicinal (a few blades of mace steeped in hot water, the water then being taken to combat nausea).

# MALDIVE FISH

Sinhalese: *umbalakada*

Dried tuna from the Maldive Islands used extensively in Sri Lankan cooking. Sold in packets, broken into small chips. Substitute dried shrimp (prawn) powder or Japanese katsuobushi.

# MINT

Bot: *Mentha viridis*
Fam: *Labiatae*
Hindi: *podina*
Sinhalese: *meenchi*
Lao: *pak hom ho*
Malay: *daun pudina*

Although there are many varieties, the common, round-leafed mint is the one most often used in cooking. It adds flavor to many curries, and mint sambal is an essential accompaniment to a "biriani" meal or as a dipping sauce for samoosa. Mint is also used in Laotian fish dishes.

# MUSHROOMS, STRAW

Bot: *Volvariella volvacea*
Burmese: *hmo*

Also known as "paddy straw mushrooms". This tiny, cultivated mushroom consists of a sheath within which is the mushroom. Available canned, bottled or dried.

# MUSTARD, BLACK

Bot: *Brassica igra*
Fam: *Crucilerae*
Hindi: *rai, kimcea* (brown mustard)
Sinhalese: *abba*
Malay: *biji sawi*

This variety of mustard seed is smaller and more pungent than the yellow variety. Substitute brown mustard seed (juncia). Alba or white mustard is not used in Asian cooking.

## NUTMEG

Bot: *Myristica fragrans*
Fam: *Myristicaceae*
Hindi: *jaiphal*
Sinhalese: *sadikka*
Malay: *buah pala*
Indonesian: *pala*

Not widely used as a curry spice, but used to flavor some sweets and cakes, and sometimes used in garam masala. For maximum flavor, always grate finely just before using. Use sparingly, for larger quantities (more than one whole nut) can be poisonous.

## ONION

Bot: *Allium cepa*
Fam: *Liliaceae*
Hindi: *peeaz*
Sinhalese: *lunu*
Malay: *bawang*
Thai: *hom hua lek*

Onions come in many varieties, but those most commonly used are the brown or white onions.

## ONION, RED

Bot: *Allium rubrum*

The most commonly used onions in Asia.

## PALM SUGAR

Hindi: *jaggery*
Sinhalese: *hakuru*
Burmese: *tanyet (palmyrah), chandagar (cane)*
Malay: *gula Melaka (Malacca) Indonesian: gula Jawa*

This strong-flavored dark sugar is obtained from the sap of coconut palms and Palmyrah palms. The sap is boiled down until it crystallizes, and the sugar is usually sold in round, flat cakes or two hemispheres put together to form a ball and wrapped in dried leaves. Substitute black sugar, an unrefined, sticky sugar sold in health food stores, or use refined dark brown sugar sold at supermarkets.

## PANCH PHORA

Panch means "five" in Hindi, and panch phora is a combination of five different aromatic seeds. These are used whole, and when added to the cooking oil impart a flavor typical of Indian food.

## PANDANUS OR SCREWPINE

Bot: *Pandanus latifolia*
Fam: *Pandanaceae*
Sinhalese: *rampé*
Thai: *bai toey*
Malay: *daun pandan*
Indonesian: *daun pandan*

Used as a flavoring in rice, curries; and as a flavoring and coloring agent in Malay and Indonesian sweets. The long, flat, green leaves are either crushed or boiled to yield the flavor and color. In Malaysia and Indonesia especially the flavor is as popular as vanilla is in the West.

## PANDANUS ODORATISSIMUS

Hindi: *kewra*

Another variety of screwpine. The male inflorescence has a stronger perfume than roses or jasmin. It is used mostly in Indian sweets, and is obtainable as an essence or concentrate. It is so strong that only a drop is needed (or, more discreetly, a small skewer dipped in the essence is swished in the liquid to be flavored). On special festive occasions, rose essence and kewra essence are used to flavor the rich rice dish, biriani.

## PEPPER, BLACK

Bot: *Piper nigrum*
Fam: *Piperaceae*
Hindi: *kali mirich*
Sinhalese: *gammiris*
Burmese: *nga-yourk-kaun*
Malay: *lada hitam*
Indonesian: *merica hitam*

Pepper, the berry of a tropical vine, is green

when immature, and red or yellow when ripe. Black pepper is obtained by sun-drying the whole berry. It is only used in some curries, but is an important ingredient in garam masala.

# PEPPER, RED & GREEN

Bot: *Capsicum grossum*
Sinhalese: *thakkali miris*

Also known as bell peppers, capsicums or sweet peppers, this large, rounded variety is very mild and sweet in flavor, and is used as a vegetable or salad ingredient.

# WHITE POPPY SEEDS

Bot: *Papaver somniferum*
Fam: *Papaveraceae*
Hindi: *khas-khas*

Used in Indian curries mainly for thickening gravies since flour, cornstarch (cornflour), or other starches are never used for thickening. The seeds are ground to a powder for this use.

# SHRIMP POWDER

Finely shredded dried shrimp (prawns), sold in packets at specialty food shops and at Chinese produce stores.

# RAMPÉ

see pandanus

# RICE, GROUND

This can be bought at many produce stores, health food stores and supermarkets, and is slightly more granular than rice flour. It gives a crisper texture when used in batters or other mixtures.

# RICE VERMICELLI

Chinese: *mei fun*
Malay: *beehoon, meehoon*
Thai: *sen mee*

Sometimes labelled "rice sticks", these are very fine rice flour noodles sold in Chinese stores. Soaking in hot water for 10 minutes prepares them sufficiently for most recipes, but in some cases they may need boiling for one or two minutes. When deep fried they swell up and turn white. For a crisp result, fry them straight from the packet without soaking.

# ROSE WATER

A very popular flavoring in Indian and Persian sweets, rose water is the diluted essence extracted from rose petals by steam distillation. If you use rose essence or concentrate, be careful not to over-flavor — count the drops. However, with rose water a tablespoon measure can be used. Buy rose water from pharmacists or from stores specialising in Asian ingredients.

# ROTI FLOUR

Creamy in color and slightly granular in texture, this is ideal flour for all unleavened breads; unlike "atta" flour, it is not made from the whole grain. Sold at some health food and Chinese stores.

# SAFFRON

Bot: *Crocus sativus*
Fam: *Iridaceae*
Hindi: *kesar*

The world's most expensive spice, saffron is obtained by drying the stamens of the saffron crocus. The thread-like strands are dark orange and have a strong perfume; it is also available in powder form. Do not confuse it with turmeric, which is sometimes sold as "Indian saffron". Beware also of cheap saffron, which in all probability will be safflower or "bastard saffron" — it looks similar, and imparts color, but has none of the authentic fragrance. Saffron is used more extensively in northern India than anywhere else in Asia.

# SAMBAL ULEK

A combination of chilies and salt, used in cooking or as an accompaniment. The old Dutch-lndonesian spelling, still seen on some labels, is "sambal oelek".

# SCALLIONS (SPRING ONIONS OR GREEN ONIONS)

Bot: *Allium cepa or Allium fistulum*
Fam: *Liliacece*

This member of the onion family is sometimes known as "shallot" in Australia, but is correctly called a spring onion almost everywhere (though the term "scallion" is popular in the USA). Spring onions are the thinnings of either *Allium cepa* or *A. fistulum* plantings that do not form a bulb. They are white and slender, with green leaves, and are used widely in China and Japan.

# SESAME SEED

Bot: *Sesamum indicum*
Fam: *Pedaliaceae*
Hindi: *till*
Sinhalese: *thala*
Malay: *bijan*

Used mostly in Korean, Chinese, and Japanese food, and in sweets in Southeast Asian countries. Black sesame, another variety known as hak chih mah (China) or kuro goma (Japan), is mainly used in the Chinese dessert, toffee apples, and as a flavoring (gomasio) mixed with salt in Japanese food.

# SESAME OIL

The sesame oil used in Chinese cooking is extracted from toasted sesame seeds, and gives a totally different flavor from the lighter-colored sesame oil sold in health food stores. For the recipes in this book, buy sesame oil from Chinese stores. Use the oil in small quantities for flavoring, not as a cooking medium.

# SHALLOTS

Bot: *Allium ascalonicum*
Fam: *Liliaceae*

Shallots are small, purplish onions with red-brown skin. Like garlic, they grow in a cluster and resemble garlic cloves in shape. In Australia the name "shallots" is generally (and incorrectly) given to spring onions or scallions.

# SHRIMP PASTE, DRIED

see Dried shrimp paste

# TAMARIND

Bot: *Tamarindus indica*
Fam: *Leguminoseae*
Hindi: *imli*
Sinhalese: *siyambala*
Malay: *asam*
Indonesian: *asam*
Thai: *som ma kham*

This acid-tasting fruit of a large tropical tree is shaped like a large lima (broad) bean and has a brittle brown shell, inside which are shiny dark seeds covered with brown flesh. Tamarind is dried, and sold in packets. For use as acid in a recipe, soak a piece the size of a walnut in $1/2$ a cup (4 fl oz, 125 ml) of hot water for 5 to 10 minutes until soft, then squeeze it until it mixes with the water and strain out the seeds and fibers. Tamarind liquid is used in given quantities.

# TURMERIC

Bot: *Curcuma longa*
Fam: *Zingiberaceae*
Hindi: *haldi*
Sinhalese: *kaha*
Burmese: *fa nwin*
Indonesian: *kunyit*
Thai: *kamin*

A rhizome of the ginger family, turmeric with its orange-yellow color is a mainstay of commercial curry powders. Though often called

Indian saffron, it should never be confused with true saffron and the two may not be used interchangeably.

# WOOD FUNGUS

Bot: *Auricalaria polytricha*

Chinese: *wun yee*

Japanese: *kikurage*

Malay: *kuping tikus*

Indonesian: *kuping jamu*

Thai: *hed henu*

Also known as "cloud ear fungus" or "jelly mushrooms", wood fungus is sold by weight, and in its dry state looks like greyish-black pieces of paper. Soaked in hot water for 10 minutes, it swells to translucent brown shapes like curved clouds or a rather prettily shaped ear – hence the name "cloud ear fungus". With its flavorless resilience it is a perfect example of a texture ingredient, adding no taste of its own but taking on subtle flavors from the foods with which it is combined. Cook only for a minute or two.

# YOGURT

Cultured yogurt. For recipes in this book, use unflavored yogurt (preferably one with a pronounced acid flavor) such as Greek yogurt or goat's milk yogurt.

# INDEX

*Seafood makes delicious curries. The recipe for this Crab Curry is on page 61.*

*Shrimp Curry from Malaysia (page 59) in its own setting.*